The Constant Leader

Also available from Network Continuum

Personalizing Learning – John West-Burnham and Max Coates

Distributing Leadership for Personalizing Learning – Ron Ritchie and
Ruth Deakin Crick

Coaching Solutions – Will Thomas and Alistair Smith

Available from Continuum

How to Run Your School Successfully – Adrian Percival and Susan Tranter

The Constant Leader

Maintaining personal effectiveness in a climate of accelerating educational change

Max Coates

Foreword by Professor Dame Pat Collarbone

network
continuum

Continuum International Publishing Group
Network Continuum
The Tower Building   80 Maiden Lane, Suite 704
11 York Road   New York, NY 10038
London
SE1 7NX

www.networkcontinuum.co.uk
www.continuumbooks.com

First published 2008
© Max Coates 2008

British Library Cataloguing-in-Publication Data
A catalogue record for this book is available from the British Library.

ISBN-13: 978 1 85539 438 4 (paperback)
ISBN-10: 1 85539 438 3 (paperback)

Library of Congress Cataloging-in-Publication Data
A catalog record for this book is available from the Library of Congress.

Typeset by Ben Cracknell Studios | www.benstudios.co.uk

Printed and bound in Great Britain by The Cromwell Press, Trowbridge, Wiltshire

Contents

Foreword by Professor Dame Pat Collarbone   vii
Introduction   ix

1   Mind the gap   1

2   The lesser-known legacy of Mr Rickenbacker   9

3   The story we find ourselves in   16

4   A peace of my mind   23

5   Values for money   33

6   It's only words   41

7   Time will tell   48

8   Tool to tyrant   55

9   Team games   62

10   The only alternative   70

11   It's not what you know but who you know   79

12   Body of knowledge   87

13   Buy one get one free   96

14   End game   104

References   112
Index   115

Foreword

Leadership of a school is possibly one of the most crucial endeavours any human being can undertake. It can also be an incredibly rewarding experience. I came to this conclusion after over six years as a headteacher of an inner-London secondary school.

For most headteachers, I believe, the moral purpose is to raise achievement in a school where children and young people, as well as staff, can feel safe and secure, despite, in some cases, very difficult circumstances. In making this a reality many of the necessary agendas do not come easily or without pain, whether they are externally or internally imposed.

For some headteachers, Max Coates suggests, the challenges may seem at times to be insurmountable. This book is designed to address some of these challenges in a sympathetic and reassuring manner. There will be headteachers who have not built an effective working relationship with their leadership team. It may well be that they think they are accountable for everything and a downturn can present itself when a mistake happens or outcomes aren't quite what was expected. A headteacher needs both challenge and support from the leadership and middle management teams he or she has helped to appoint. Headteachers who are new to the post must ensure trust is developed quickly so that they are in a position to move the school forward.

Some headteachers appear confident and on top of this challenging role. In my experience, they still make mistakes, often can't sleep at night and worry that they are failing either their pupils or their staff. This book is also for those headteachers who we believe are exemplary but who still have those 'nagging' doubts. And, finally, there are those headteachers or those aspiring to headship who are doing a competent job, have the confidence of their leadership team and staff but who continue to doubt their own abilities.

So why read this book? It is written by someone who has spent many years as a headteacher. More importantly, it is written by someone who has spent several years addressing the key concerns headteachers may face. Max is an experienced leadership and management consultant and this publication provides welcome and timely leadership advice. One of Max's key points is that a headteacher needs a mentor, someone who will challenge his or her actions honestly but who is also a pillar of support. For me, the arrival of a mentor changed my life in a very positive way.

Too often a headteacher can believe he or she is expected to know the answers to every question and therefore expected to know the solution. In a time of turbulent change this concept is very misleading. Max addresses this point 'head on' and deals with both the emotional and the political results. This is a welcome leadership book designed to help headteachers survive and flourish.

Professor Dame Pat Collarbone

Introduction

It is hard to believe that we have reached the twentieth anniversary of the Education Reform Act (1988). This Act provided the framework for so much of our current educational landscape including local management of schools and the National Curriculum. At its heart was a belief that a centralized approach to schooling would be beneficial. The imposition of such a model offered an illusion of stability by reducing school-by-school differences. In reality many of those who have led our schools over the past twenty years have found themselves worn down by the relentless change that they were required to implement. It is a sobering thought that none of our educational workforce under the age of forty has known any other context.

The year following this anniversary presents a less palatable milestone. The National College for School Leadership (2006) finds that 2009 marks the start of a seven-year high in terms of headteacher retirements and an exacerbation in shortages of senior leaders in our schools. This same document shows that re-advertising unfilled vacancies alone cost £1 million in 2005. There is also a lack of enthusiasm from 'other ranks' to step into these freshly vacated shoes. One survey cites a figure of 43 per cent of deputies not wanting to take this next career step (NCSL, 2006).

Faced with a looming crisis the Department for Education and Skills (2007) commissioned a review of school leadership by PricewaterhouseCoopers. The report concludes that there are:

> a number of key challenges for school leadership as we move forward into the 21st century. Many of the challenges faced by school leaders today are driven by the increase in the scale and complexity of agendas that school leaders are having to take forward. A large part of this is driven by the changes associated with the juxtaposition, through Every Child Matters, of the learning and standards agendas on the one hand, and the social and inclusion agendas on the other. In addition, as we have outlined in the Report, other major policy initiatives including the 14–19 agenda and BSF, all present their own particular challenges for school leaders going forward. All of this means that schools and schooling are changing radically, and this in turn poses a fundamentally different set of challenges for school leadership (although the ultimate aim of promoting better outcomes and standards for children and young people remains). (page 177)

The report is limited in that it offers such a narrow focus on the role of school leadership. The conception of the future is an extended version of the present and leadership is about extending capacity. The report fails to explore the leadership required to address the deeper and pervasive changes, which are shaping both our society and education. It is more about function than about reviewing the essential qualities of leaders who will be the fulcrum of innovative change. Educational leadership viewed in this way is analogous to being chased by a pack of wolves towards a cliff edge (I will deal with the power of positive imagery in a later chapter!). The PricewaterhouseCoopers report seems to engage with the wolves but not the increasingly imminent precipice.

This book seeks to look at how leaders retain purpose under pressure and, crucially, lever the considerable skills and talent in their schools to create a long overdue educational futurescape. Leadership in any form can be exhilarating and empowering. Handled wrongly it can be self-destructive and also damaging to those around. This book is about skiing down the black-runs of leadership without being taken off-piste by air ambulance.

Chapter 1 explores leadership in a society in transition. Chapter 2 looks at the constant impact of emotional communication, both the leader's impact in shaping the school and those in the school's role in shaping the leader's emotions. Chapter 3 explores the idea of a perception as a construct and how a negative view changes everything. Chapter 4 considers the power of the emotional brain and what happens when it comes into conflict with the cognitive brain and the dangers that ensue. Chapter 5 focuses on values and what happens when practice and belief become misaligned. Chapter 6's words say it all but many of these are used in self-talk, which needs assessment and modification. Chapter 7 reviews effective time management whilst Chapter 8 takes this further into the area of IT. Chapter 9 considers teams, which can increase capacity and effectiveness but which can also be time wasting and a locus of stress for their members. Chapter 10 explores problem solving and creative thinking. Chapter 11 highlights the need to manage knowledge as it explodes and what a learning organization might look like. Chapter 12 looks at bodily heath as a requisite for leadership. Chapter 13 explores the potential impact and demands of system leadership. Chapter 14, the final chapter, is about developing an action plan to turn theory into practice for leaders.

I am grateful for the support and conversations with so many people. I would particularly like to mention Douglas Archibald, Professor Dame Pat Collarbone, Professor Peter Earley, Dr John Eaton, Alan Flintham, Barrie Joy, Dr Steve Sparks and Professor John West-Burnham. Their contributions were extremely useful; the mistakes, however, are all mine. Many thanks are also due to the staff at Continuum, especially Bridget Gibbs.

Special thanks are due to my wife Sally and my sons David, Matt and Steve, who have lived through the gestation of this book during many meals and remained largely gracious about the project.

1 Mind the gap

We are at that very point in time when a four-hundred-year-old age is rattling in its deathbed and another is struggling to be born. (Hock, 1999, page 10)

Bob Dylan's iconic 1960s song 'The Times They Are A-Changin' identified endemic change. It is, however, unlikely that he had a truly prophetic grasp of the enormity of what he was describing. For many people, change is about life becoming faster, louder and brighter. Arguably, what we are experiencing at the present time is something more radical, namely transition. Unpredictably, events conspire to change the way society understands itself and operates. Dee Hock, founder and ex-CEO of Visa, extends his view thus:

A shifting of culture, science, society and institutions enormously greater and swifter than the world has ever experienced. Ahead, lies the possibility of regeneration of individuality, liberty, community and ethics such as the world has never known, and a harmony with nature, with one another and with the divine intelligence such as the world has never seen. It is the path to a livable future in the centuries ahead, as society evolves into ever-increasing diversity and complexity. (Hock, 1999, page 10)

The earlier four-hundred-year-old breakpoint referred to is the transition from the medieval period to the enlightenment. The former was a period where the prevailing worldview, whether expressed in terms of cosmology or of social organization, was one of finite boundaries perceived as being imposed by divine purpose. The enlightenment, on the other hand, assumed a paradigm of human optimism with unfettered learning establishing truth, understanding and the solution to human problems. This transitional point was not like seeing in the New Year with one age passing and a new one starting with the chiming of a clock. The reality was messy and most present would be unaware that they were at a defining point.

Hock's argument is that we are at another fork in the road of human history, though it is not the intention of this book to explore this change in detail. The following are offered as indicators and not definitions of this transition:

- The development of communications in terms of both speed and personal access.
- Globalization with its 24/7 engagement and wakefulness.
- A lack of confidence in a mechanistic worldview as the indeterminacy of post-Einsteinian theories of relativity has become assimilated into popular thinking (just think of *Dr Who*). The subplot is that even science is not as straightforward as we thought it was and is definitely not as reliable!
- Institutional authority is being freely challenged whether political, in our schools or at our health centres and hospitals.
- The ownership of knowledge and learning has broken through established protocols and elites.

The previous quotation by Dee Hock is optimistic but a positive outcome is not certain and he offers a further, bleaker scenario:

> Unfortunately, ahead lies equal possibility of massive institutional failure, enormous social carnage and regression to that ultimate manifestation of Newtonian, mechanistic concepts of organization, dictatorship, which, in turn, would have to collapse with even more carnage before new concepts of organization could emerge. (Hock, 1999, page 11)

Without wishing to labour the point, our world has changed and has done so at an exponential rate. Understanding context is hugely important, as a walk past houses in Venice would quickly establish. To give another example, the emergence of China as the workshop of the world has huge implications for our society, economy and our schools especially in the area of curriculum design and development. Fifty years ago 80 per cent of the population made or moved something; now it is less than 10 per cent, with most of the workforce actually making their jobs up as they go along. Generating workers for the leisure and tourism industries can soak up only so many of the industrially dispossessed. Much of our current planning in education still seems to assume that the future will be a modified version of the past. Such a view is a triumph of optimism over reality.

Consider for a moment the implications of just two of the areas that have been highlighted as drivers of this change in worldview: communication and the ownership of knowledge and learning.

The speed of change in technology is legend. Around 1951 Professor Douglas Hartree concluded:

> All the calculations that would ever be needed in this country could be done on the three digital computers, which were then being built – one in Cambridge, one in Teddington, and one in Manchester. No one else, he said, would ever need machines of their own, or would be able to afford to buy them. (Bowden, 1969, page 2)

In 1949 *Popular Mechanics* magazine prophesied that 'in the future computers will weigh just below 1.5 tons'. Clearly such predictions were myopic.

In 1970 Alvin Toffler wrote *Future Shock*, which identified the impact of the changes resulting from burgeoning knowledge and high-speed connectivity between people and organizations. *Future Shock* sold over six million copies; intriguingly it was an extension of an article originally written for *Playboy* magazine. Alvin and Heidi Toffler (2006) have updated their assessment in *Revolutionary Wealth*, in which they point out that the pace of change is unabated. The following are quotations which capture how quickly today becomes yesterday.

- Today there are more than 800,000,000 PCs on the planet – one for every seven or eight human beings.
- Today there are well over 500 billion computer chips on the planet. Many contain more than 100 million transistors – on-off switches – and Hewlett Packard announces it has found a way to put billions or even trillions of 'molecular-size' on-off switches on a single tiny chip.
- Today an estimated 100 billion ever-more-powerful chips deluge the market per year.
- In 2002 the Japanese built a computer called the Earth Simulator designed to help forecast global climate changes. It performed 40,000 billion calculations per second – faster than its seven closest rivals combined. By 2005, IBM had reclaimed the lead with a supercomputer twice as fast, and scientists predict that computers may reach petaflop speeds – a thousand trillion mathematical operations a second – by the end of the decade.
- Meanwhile, the number of Internet users worldwide is estimated at between 700,000,000 and 900,000,000.
- Vietnam hopes its software sales will top $500,000,000 in five years.
- Brazil counts over 14,000,000 Internet users. (page 6)

- In principle, researchers can – or soon will be able to – 'walk around' inside a single grain of rice to visually observe how its internal structures morph as it grows, then continue to watch them as the rice is stored, processed, shipped, and cooked. Researchers will be able, as it were, to stroll through an intestine as it digests the rice.
- But faster is astonishingly slow when it comes to nuclear physics. To study the erratic motion of individual electrons as they circle the nucleus of an atom, researchers need to fire extremely short bursts of electromagnetic radiation. The briefer the better. Recently Dutch and French laser scientists broke records by creating pulses of strobe light lasting no more than 220 attoseconds – i.e., 220 billionths of a billionth of a second. But to study what happens inside the nucleus, even that is too slow. So American researchers have been working on a 'Lasetron' designed to create flashes measured in zeptoseconds – billionths of a trillionth of a second. (page 7)

The numbers quoted above simply startle but do not actually make the nature of change comprehensible. It is apparent, however, that the enormity and complexity of knowledge creation and communication is no longer rooted in the printed page in the hands of a minority of users. The World Wide Web with its associated infrastructure has created new ways of learning and knowledge creation. Users of the internet are no longer content to be an audience but are participants. This movement from consumers of information to creators of knowledge is perfectly illustrated by the phenomenon of Wikipedia, the online encyclopedia.

In 1768 the first edition of the *Encyclopedia Britannica* was published. In fact initial articles started to appear in December of that year and finally ran to 2,391 pages in three volumes by 1771. Knowledge was systematically arranged in a manner which rapidly became a 'gold standard'. Some would even argue that this structure, born all those years ago in Edinburgh, is the basis of the National Curriculum today. Other encyclopedias followed, eventually making the transition on to the web. Encarta is probably the best known with 36,000 articles in 2006; it is a closed product, part of the Microsoft stable, and produced by commissioned contributors.

Contrast this with Wikipedia, which has one employee, thousands of volunteer contributors and 1,736,564 articles in April 2007. In theory anyone can contribute or edit these. At this juncture many people have voiced concerns about the reliability of its content, especially as it is probably the most extensively used resource for school projects. It is 'the people's encyclopedia' policed by a process of peer review. Of course it is not necessarily 'experts' who write the content and there is no true editorial board. There have been significant failures but then the traditional method of knowledge management has not been above reproach either. Tim Radford (2003) writing in the *Guardian* found little difficulty in identifying 50 scientific hoaxes. Ironically he placed the psychologist Sir Cyril Burt at number 4. Burt had been hugely influential in establishing the 11-plus selection process; his foundational work on IQ was shown to be not only statistically flawed but also that he had fabricated the names of some of his researchers.

The importance of Wikipedia is that it has relocated knowledge and learning outside the 'authorized' structures. It also places the control of content and process with the learners.

> ICT has introduced an anarchic element into education where the students are more proficient in its use than many of those teaching. It subverts the learning order from knowledge transmission to personalized-knowledge creation. Regrettably, the students have not fully grasped the existing rules of the game and have become cognitively free-range. (West-Burnham and Coates, 2005, page 95)

It is a fascinating thought that there are teaching staff using interactive whiteboards in classrooms who can remember being taught with a personal slate and chalk. Most of the really significant changes in ICT have taken place during the schooling of those currently in sixth forms.

Leading through transition

Our current understanding of school leadership has evolved against this backdrop of transition. During periods of rapid change, uncertainty and innovation, confident leaders become highly prized. An individual who has a map of the territory, or at least who claims to have one, is frequently welcomed by those making appointments to senior leadership positions.

This situation underpinned the David Blunkett initiative that linked 'fresh start schools' with the appointment of 'superheads'. Spawned in 1997 it became a source of embarrassment and disappointment when three of the initial ten 'superheads' resigned in rapid succession in 2000. Subsequently one of these three, the head of the Islington Arts and Media School, Torsten Friedag, was the centrepiece of a BBC2 documentary (2000) entitled *Head on the Block*. In a review of this three-part television series Mark Lawson (2000) writing in the *Guardian* commented:

> Head On The Block is a triumph for BBC2 but may also solve a problem at the neighbouring channel. The job of Controller is virtually impossible in the current environment and many have failed at it. But Torsten Friedag – his idealism apparently unbroken – is probably the only person in the country who would willingly agree to run BBC1.

Lawson's tongue-in-cheek assessment of Friedag was as a man who did not recognize his own limits and who had either considerable self-confidence or a level of optimism that was wholly unrealistic.

Michael Maccoby (2001) explored aspects of leadership by drawing on Freud. Whilst there are an infinite number of personalities he identified three main types: erotic, obsessive and narcissistic. These provide a useful analysis of leadership, though it has to be admitted that they do carry a lot of 'baggage'. Describing yourself as an erotic leader may do wonders for your self-esteem; however, it could lead to problems if used as a descriptor in your CV.

'Erotic' is not used here in a sexual sense but in terms of a personality type who seeks to love and be loved. A person dominant in this category tends to emphasize the care of others. As managers they are usually supportive but likely to avoid even necessary conflict and as a result find making decisions difficult where people are involved. Leaders with an emphatic obsessive personality type are likely to be inner-directed and conscientious. They have an eye for detail and usually have exacting standards. The negative side of this personality type is that they are inclined to be risk averse and often perceived as a little slow.

The third category of leaders, those with the narcissistic personality dimension, tends to be innovators who are often driven with an eye on the power and the glory. Central to their motivation is a desire to be admired rather than loved. Productive narcissists often define and present vision very effectively. Frequently they are inspirational orators, believing that words can move mountains. Churchill and John F. Kennedy would both serve as excellent examples.

We have elements of all three personality types, which are perhaps best pictured as the points of an isosceles triangle. However, any one of the three can be dominant and sometimes to an extreme and unhelpful degree. Our triangle would then become skewed (see Figures 1.1 and 1.2).

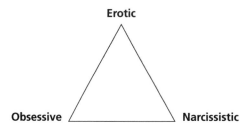

Figure 1.1 The balanced leader

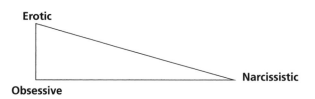

Figure 1.2 The narcissistic leader

It is the narcissistic leader who is most likely to claim to have the 'map' and the most likely personality type to be represented amongst a group of 'superheads'. This tends to correlate with the individual who defaults to a pacesetting or commanding leadership style. These styles are outlined in greater detail by Goleman et al. (2002). Narcissistic leaders can impress, and indeed many interviewing panels have been swayed in their favour by their confidence and apparent sense of purpose and vision.

There is a dark side to narcissistic leaders, which, if it is pronounced, can result in creating bigger issues in an organization than the ones that they were brought in to resolve. These are so-called unproductive narcissists, who have a number of key traits: they are unlikely to listen, empathy will be in short supply, and paradoxically they are extremely sensitive to criticism though they will take little notice of its substance. They will often take credit for the work of subordinates, and tend to be very competitive. Crucially it is usually in their success that the seeds of subsequent failure are likely to be sown. As they achieve success they can become increasingly confident and ever more prone to take risks. By this stage they often begin to surround themselves with sycophants, having forced out key players who might offer legitimate challenge. This is a very dangerous and volatile mix and often the point at which those who have made the appointment start to become uneasy.

Narcissistic leaders tend to speak enthusiastically of teamwork but have no commitment to working this way. In fact they want an audience not a team. In running team programmes over the past five years it has usually been the narcissistic heads who presented the single most significant obstacle to the development of teams.

The principal arguments of this chapter are that first, at this transitional point education is radically transforming in terms of content and process, with the latter becoming increasingly important. Second, individual leaders cannot have the range of knowledge or skills to generate and implement new models for learning and knowledge management. It would be inappropriate to define the required leadership as a stereotype; however, the following qualities are more than desirable and should be viewed as essential:

- cognizance of the nature of change at national and global levels;
- fascination by and engagement with new developments in learning being generated by neurological research;
- commitment to innovation but not novelty;
- security with personal values;
- a team player at the level of both the institution and the system;
- understanding of knowledge to be held by the community and not by the individual;
- development of conscious strategies to build succession;
- commitment to personal lifelong learning;
- an able communicator though not necessarily an orator;
- understanding of the nature and importance of teams and strategies for building and maintaining these;
- empathy – a person who listens to empower others;
- a reflective practitioner who can receive and utilize feedback;
- capacity to sustain positive leadership in the face of pressure and who understands both threat and opportunity in initiating and leading change.

Designing the future is the collective endeavour of the many not the vision of the few. Our rapidly changing context requires radical innovation or we will not be able to create and sustain an economically viable post-industrial society. In 1970 Alvin Toffler concluded: 'The illiterate of the 21st century will not be those who cannot read and write, but those who cannot learn, unlearn, and relearn.'

Just thinking

In 1910 Sheffield Simplex Motor Company produced a car intended to rival the Rolls Royce. My great uncle Jim was given the task of demonstrating its reliability and flexibility by driving one of these cars, with its transmission locked in top gear, from Land's End to John o'Groats without stalling it. He came up behind a slow-moving farm cart, which would have caused him to stop and stall, burst through a five-barred gate and drove round a field until the escort vehicle could clear the way forward. Spectators viewed this exploit with attitudes ranging from incredulity to ridicule. At this point the horse drawn vehicle was at the zenith of its development whereas the car was in its infancy. The former offered security and predictability; the latter unreliability but a glimpse of the future.

Arguably we are witnessing many schools at the peak of their development. A good example of this is the 'Building Schools for the Future' initiative, which has made a significant impact upon our ageing school stock. However, the question being asked by many educationalists is about the appropriateness of conventional schools and even their survival in the future. They are often built with limited revision of design whilst students' learning is becoming less contained and increasingly pursued through a free-ranging, virtual, 24/7 environment. It may well be that the perceptions of the horse and car in the early part of the twentieth century provide a powerful metaphor for the development of learning in the twenty-first century, when schools are becoming more polished whilst alternatives still look somewhat obscure and even fanciful.

At the time of writing many people are becoming aware that the rate of change has become all-pervading. Some find this empowering; others feel a profound sense of unease. The following chapters seek to support and equip leaders in creating learning processes for the future whilst retaining personal perspective, equanimity and health.

2 The lesser-known legacy of Mr Rickenbacker

Smiles have the edge over all other emotional expressions: the human brain prefers happy faces, recognizing them more readily and quickly that those with negative expressions – an effect known as the 'happy face advantage'. (Goleman, 2006, page 44)

Man seems to be capable of great virtues but not of small virtues; capable of defying his torturer but not of keeping his temper. (G.K. Chesterton)

Resonance and induction

If you hold a stringed instrument when a musical note is sounded nearby its strings will vibrate in sympathy if they are of the same pitch. The string is said to resonate. The inclusion of the guitar in bands in the first part of the twentieth century presented a problem in that it could not compete with the volume of the other instruments. In 1931 George Beauchamp and an engineer, Adolph Rickenbacker, produced the first electric guitar, which allowed the string movement to be captured and amplified. This was achieved using a guitar and bits out of a sewing machine motor (apparently the washing machine components proved to be too large!). It harnessed the idea that a metal string vibrating across the pole piece of an electro-magnet produces a small electrical current. This in turn could be amplified. The production of the current from the movement of the string is known as induction. The guitar was now amplified and had found a voice and it was the other instruments that were now trying to compete.

This information could significantly enhance your credibility with teenage card-carrying guitarists. Of greater importance is that it provides a useful metaphor for human communication. Consider two people engaged in a conversation. This is not simply an exchange of words or ideas; there is a more primal process taking place. Our emotional state is usually portrayed in our body language and in our facial expression in particular.

One person responds to the state being expressed, resonating, in other words, like the string on the instrument. Conversely, that person has emotions expressed through his or her own body language and facial expressions and in turn engenders emotions in the first person like the string inducing a current in Rickenbacker's guitar pick-up.

To a large extent this seems a statement of the obvious. We know a pleasant expression can disarm the malignant, and conversely the headteacher walking through the school with a look like Genghis Khan on an off-day can send out ripples of alarm to staff and students. The argument here is that the whole area of facial expression is more sophisticated than many have recognized and that our facial expression engenders emotion not only with others but also within ourselves. Further, that leadership has a significant emotional dimension. When the leader is displaying 'calm under fire' or maintaining the appearance of confidence when problems seem to be overwhelming, this comes with a large personal price tag.

Paul Ekman and Wallace Friesen (1978) concluded that the facial muscles could generate 43 distinct movements or action units. In turn these could be combined to provide thousands of combinations. They decided that not all of these had meaning but certainly those that did ran into nearly three thousand. These are detailed in the Facial Action Coding System (FACS). Ekman's work shows that the face has a very wide repertoire of expressions and that it is an extremely rich source of information on emotions. Those proficient in the use of FACS can operate almost as if they have the ability to read minds. Certainly they can usually detect lies. Capturing facial expressions in slow motion using video will often reveal micro-second giveaways in people's expressions that occur before they have their faces back under control again! Of course one disadvantage for the non-expert is that this whole process is taking place at great speed, often subliminally. The result is that we sense some of the messages coming from the other person but may fail to interpret them. Ekman's meticulous work on facial expression has also been used to enhance computer animations such as *Toy Story* and *Shrek*.

Many would feel fairly comfortable with the idea of the face or perhaps the eyes being a window to the mind. Ekman and Friesen found that facial expression in turn changed their emotions. They discovered that adopting certain muscle configurations induced the associated emotion, for example sadness, anguish or anger. In 1988 psychologist Fritz Strack of the University of Würzburg, Germany, asked two groups of people to judge how funny they found some cartoons. In one group, participants held a pencil between their teeth without its touching their lips, which forced a smile. The other group was asked to hold the pencil with their lips but not using their teeth, forcing a frown. The results revealed that people experience the emotion associated with their expressions: those with a forced smile felt happier, and found the cartoons funnier than those who were forced to frown. At this point the caveat should be made that inducing a friendly ethos in a school is probably better without pencils.

The discovery (initially in higher primates and then in humans) of two distinctive types of nerve cells, mirror neurons and spindle cells, has paved the way for a greater understanding of such human interactions. Mirror neurons allow us to mimic the actions of other people including, significantly, facial expressions and help us understand the other person's intentions. Exposure to the emotions of others will generate neurological responses in our own brains similar to theirs. Goleman (2006) argues that:

> Mirror neurons make emotions contagious, letting the feelings we witness flow through us, helping us get in synch and follow what's going on. We 'feel' the other in the broadest sense of the word: sensing their sentiments, their movements, their sensations, their emotions as they act inside us. (page 42)

Spindle cells are found in abundance in humans certainly when contrasted with the numbers found in other primates. They are relatively large and provide a superhighway across particular parts of the brain, including the limbic centre, which is a key part of the emotional brain or 'bodymind'. This is discussed in more detail in Chapter 4. There is then linkage with the anterior cingulated cortex (ACC), the area of the brain that directs our attention and coordinates our thoughts and emotions. It is the ACC that guides our recognition of facial expression and is certainly active when we feel emotion. There is also connection through these spindle cells to the orbitofrontal area of the prefrontal cortex (OFC). This area is the lowest part of the thinking brain with nerve projections coming from the eyes. The OFC is again involved in our emotional reactions to others such as an infant crying or sensing sadness in someone we care about.

In essence we have a radar system that is identifying the body and facial language of another. This leads in turn to understanding of the other and is part of the process of anticipating another's intentions. The previously mentioned spindle cells make this extremely fast. The speed of operation of the limbic centre, where much of this is activity is embedded, frequently leaves the cognitive brain struggling to keep up.

I know just how you feel

Empathy at its most basic is about high-quality communication, about engaging at a profound level with someone else. It requires us to make time and space to allow our bodymind or emotional brain to observe the body language and facial expressions of another and then through modelling expressions begin to understand something of where that person is. As you then model emotions he or she will feel heard and valued and this will enhance communication. It is OK to defer a conversation with a colleague because you do not have time; it is not satisfactory to pretend that you have the time and then short-change the other person. Indeed it is not acceptable that we are short-changed either.

In schools many conversations of significance are still inappropriately carried out 'on the run' in corridors.

It is this ability of our brains to read and mimic the expressions of another that seems to be at the root of empathy.

This is quite distinct from sympathy. I would argue that sympathy is largely about pulling out our own related memories and then immersing ourselves in the linked emotional memories that come attached. The fallacy of this is that we can only ever have similar experiences but never ones that are exactly the same. That phrase 'I know just how you feel', whilst well meant, is actually an insult. It implies that your experience is more important and blocks us from understanding what the other person is really communicating.

At the heart of empathic communication is listening. This is one of the biggest gifts that we can give another. There are of course different levels of listening and it is only at the fourth level that empathy commences at any meaningful level. The following are useful indicators to how we are listening to another person:

- *Hearing* – we hear sounds but not words. It is typified by the description of the other person 'droning on'.
- *Listening to* – there is real listening taking place, what is being said is being understood. In reality at this level we are looking for connection points in the conversation where we can interject our contribution, often as a view, a story or an anecdote.
- *Listening for* – again, words are being heard and understood. It is the motivation here that is crucial; there is an element of judgement or seeking confirmation of our assessment of the situation. Consider this listening style in the context of performance management. The listener has a view or a judgement and is waiting to hear information to substantiate that opinion.
- *Deep listening* – here, full attention is given to the speaker by the listener. There is a commitment to understand at many levels. Three factors significantly support deep listening: first, a stilling of our own inner dialogue, which may range from devising a shopping list to even rehearsing that clever question that you got on that coaching course. Second, assume a relaxed posture, preferably seated with your shoulders lowered; posture helps to engage the bodymind and thus additional listening resources. Third, soften your focus and let your eyes take in the whole person. The last factor is particularly important for men, who tend to operate with a more limited visual field.

> Listening well has been found to distinguish the best managers, teachers and leaders. Among those in the helping professions, like physicians and social workers, such deep listening numbers among the top three abilities of those whose work has been rated as outstanding by their organizations. Not only do they take the time to listen and so attune to the other person's feelings; they also ask questions to better understand the person's background situation – not just the immediate problem or diagnosis at hand. (Goleman, 2006, page 88)

Interaction

Case study: Engagement

Dr Terry Fish is the head of Twynham School, Dorset. This is a very highly rated school of some fifteen-hundred pupils. I followed him for the first two hours of a 'normal' school day recording his interactions. These were crudely divided into verbal and non-verbal.

This was an intriguing two hours following a consummate professional about his daily business. In the period 249 interactions were recorded of which 131 involved a verbal interchange whilst 118 were limited to a glance, a smile or a wave; certainly there was eye contact.

What emerged strongly was the wide range of encounters and the very rapid transition from the trivial to the complex and back again. Discussions in the period included finances, student behaviour, uniform, damage to bicycles, exclusions, school organization and, perhaps unusually, the progress of the school's tortoises (presumably slow?). The observation session included 14 minutes of non-engagement with people whilst emails were answered. The remainder of the time was very intensive.

Terry is very sensitive to school climate and ethos and many of these interchanges with people were encouraging and supportive. Each person or group was scanned and read and responses made that consistently supported the intended ethos.

At this point it is valuable to consider the case study above. The headteacher was considered to be positive and encouraging, perceived as an approachable and transparent person. Arguably this activity is hugely demanding in terms of the energy required; each person is subconsciously scanned and responded to with a smile or a comment. The scanning process is also warning whether contact with members of the school community will result in receiving an accolade or an ambush, a bouquet or a brickbat. If there are ongoing problems in the school or difficulties with particular individuals then the level of alertness will increase.

This apparently routine activity is actually quite draining. As a head I viewed walking the school as almost 'recreational'. It provided an opportunity to get away from the phone and computer and also to enjoy some brief exercise after periods of physical inaction sat at a desk. Terry Fish was engaged in 131 verbal interactions in two hours. That is a rate of more than one per second (some were, of course, to small groups).

Perhaps the zenith of interpersonal interactions is the assembly. Some years ago I was deputy head at a school where space restrictions meant that many of these gatherings were held in the playground. The head, an ex-naval officer, had the whole school stand to attention and then before starting the assembly itself they were permitted to stand 'at ease'. I want to make it clear for reasons of personal vanity that this was 1990 not 1890. On one occasion I had to announce the tragic death of a pupil. It was extremely unsettling to experience the whole school community go very still and totally quiet before I had even spoken. This is the power of induction; my body language and facial expression had made a statement that something very serious was about to be said. Six hundred people immediately understood the gravity of the situation simultaneously. Many will have experienced similar events and it is a powerful illustration of the impact of non-verbal communication.

The fallacy of the open door

A number of leaders attempt to make a statement about the transparency of their leadership style by stating that they operate an 'open door policy'. This is probably best described as well intentioned but foolhardy. The effectiveness of the leader is more likely to be enhanced by rationing contact.

The following are frequently observed interaction styles within schools:

- *Silent wonder* – some heads do not engage and can be perceived as distant and remote. It is unlikely that they are fully aware of what is happening within the school. Further, they are unlikely to build quality relationships, which underpin so many crucial leadership activities.
- *Gushing* – this is often stress related. Details of recent events are offloaded, often at random. The essential difficulty with this approach is that other people are being used as receptacles and their needs and views are not sought. In the jargon it is asymmetric communication.
- *Plastic* – this approach is characterized by a lack of authenticity. Staff are left feeling that comment and praise are being given because this comes 'with the job' and should be done rather than because it is a genuine response. This is a particular issue with narcissistic leaders.
- *Escaped prisoner* – sometimes leaders prowl the school and engage in conversation because what is in their office is to be avoided. In essence it is a displacement activity in the 'not urgent and not important' category.
- *The devil's in the detail* – a common response with obsessive, detail-driven leaders. The conversation is about the minutiae of their current task and possibly your interaction with it. Again the conversation tends to be egocentric.
- *Over-engaged* – the leader is well intentioned but does not have the balance right. There is an excessive interest in the activities of the person that he or she is communicating with.
- *Professional* – the leader engages in sincere and relevant conversation. Listening is part of the interaction and there are cues dropped which show that the leader is aware of the other person's role and activity within the school.

Leadership is a core task within any school. It is said that the only people who make more decisions per unit time than secondary headteachers are air traffic controllers! The operational activity of many headteachers is perhaps best described as relentless. Activities need to be scheduled and not slotted in around interruptions. The senior leaders are there as just that; they are required to engage in the task of leadership. A constant check is needed to ensure that they are engaged with the 'urgent and important' and the strategic thinking implicit in the 'not urgent but important'. They are not there primarily as customer service executives or even counsellors.

3 The story we find ourselves in

History is the version of past events that people have decided to agree upon.
(Napoleon Bonaparte)

We are hard-wired to tell stories. Alan Flintham (2003a), in research for *Reservoirs of Hope*, found headteachers desperate to share their narratives. At a more mundane level, just stand in the queue in the building society or post office and listen. Relatively few customers limit themselves to a simple transaction; many embellish the fiscal exchange with stories about their journey, the weather, grandchildren and even their health (or more usually its deficiency). Post-toddling children delight in transfixing consenting adults with accounts of their exploits.

So why are stories so germane to human existence? There are probably two major drivers: first, our need for significance or context and second, the need to order or make sense of our private world.

Do you know who I am?

When people meet they try to find connection with each other. Consider for a moment going to a party. As strangers meet, questions flow. 'How do you know Jim and Betty?' 'What do you do for a living?' 'Do you play golf?' and 'Have you got any children?' If connection is made through these questions and the subsequent storytelling the embryonic relationship continues. If the links are not made then the individuals move on to other victims of relentless enquiry. We like people who are like us or people who are like who we would like to emulate. In a recent conversation with Steve Denning he suggested that 'dogs sniff each other and humans tell stories'.

We believe that we are connected, if not directly then at the distance of a few interpersonal steps. This idea came from the work of psychologist Stanley Milgram. He randomly selected the names of 160 people living in Omaha, Nebraska and sent each one a packet with the name and address of a stockbroker who worked in Boston and lived in Sharon, Massachusetts. They were asked to put their own name on the packet and then mail it to someone they knew who was closer geographically. When the packet arrived Milgram noted how many people had been involved in the chain. Typically most packets involved a chain of some five or six individuals. It is from this experiment that we get the idea of six degrees of separation and lends some substance to the view that it is indeed a small world.

Stories and their truncated relatives, anecdotes, are the vehicles for establishing connection. Paradoxically, excessively complex, disconnected or long-drawn-out stories break connections between people.

My perception is my reality

Case study: Reframing

Alex had been the deputy head of a large comprehensive for six years. He was recognized as a 'safe pair of hands' and in particular as a competent manager with a good eye for detail.

The headteacher had retired and an initial recruitment process had failed to find a suitable replacement. The departing head had run the school in an autocratic manner using a process of paternalism, unpredictability and volcanic outbursts to control staff and students alike. He was a man who enjoyed bad relationships.

Alex was asked by the governing body to run the school until a replacement could be appointed. It looked as if resolution could be some way off in the future and support was offered in the form of a mentor. The mentoring process focused on exploring the change between being predominantly a manager to developing as a leader. Processes for generating vision, teamworking and motivation were also considered.

The mentor noticed a marked change between two consecutive sessions. These were three weeks apart. The first was optimistic with a realistic recognition of key challenges notably centred on reducing a deficit budget and staffing issues. The second session was pessimistic. The issues which were previously seen as a challenge and forum to demonstrate leadership skills were now perceived as insurmountable, Relationships with other senior colleagues and governors were taken as a conspiracy set up to undermine his efforts. Application for the headship was perceived as a futile gesture and not worth the effort.

What had changed? In objective terms very little. The budget deficit, created largely by the ineptitude of his predecessor, was history and not breaking news. No one had challenged the idea of his applying for the headship; indeed a number of people continued to encourage him. The largely dysfunctional leadership team was running true to form after a number of years of working under a divide and rule strategy.

Probing revealed that there had been a difficult governors' meeting. High on the agenda was the budget. The finance 'supremo' amongst the governors had not had time to digest the revised budget and its approval was delayed. In turn this had a significant impact on staffing decisions. There had been neither ownership of the issues nor recognition that they had been bullied into approving poor financial decisions by the previous head. There had also been a difficult conversation with another senior leader who had been an acolyte of his predecessor and who was not enjoying the chill wind of responsibility.

The mentor challenged Alex's perception of events, in particular asking what had actually changed. The views of the recalcitrant colleague were also explored and it was concluded that his main virtue was actually consistency! Language was explored. Phrases such as 'They have all got it in for me', 'I'm not respected in this role' and 'There is no way they would appoint me as head' were challenged.

By the end of the session Alex had recognized that the biggest change in the past three weeks was his perception. He reframed this and his world changed. In particular his language became less extreme and ambiguity was now allowable. Positive comments were now accepted and between this session and the next he ceased to focus on collecting negative data for writing the script for his own personal 'disaster movie'.

The second driver of our need to tell stories relates to the ordering of our private world. We frequently define this by telling stories. Many people struggle with the idea of their experience being considered in these terms. They believe that their account of the world is stable, objective and corresponds with the experience of others. In fact nothing could be further from the truth. Our perception is our reality and is a highly edited version of our engagement with the world we inhabit. There is usually a working congruence between our story and other people's versions of events. It is this overlap that allows communication and common enterprise.

The story we live in has an extremely significant impact on the way in which we think. Our ordering of our experience changes the way in which we perform, how we process challenge, how we make decisions, the information that we collect and even our physiology at the cellular level throughout our bodies. Candace Pert (1997) commented:

It's well documented, for example, that people have more heart attacks on Monday mornings (when the work week begins) than any other day of the week, and that death rates peak during the days after Christmas for Christians and after Chinese New Year for the Chinese. Since these are all days with high emotional valence, one way or another, it seems clear that the emotions in some way correlate with the state of people's hearts. (page 189)

Our mental state does indeed affect performance. Dutch researchers Dijksterhuis and van Knippenberg (1998) asked a group of students to answer 42 questions taken from the game 'Trivial Pursuit'. Before answering the questions half were asked to think about soccer hooligans and the other half about university professors. They were allotted five minutes and asked to write down what came to mind. Immediately afterwards they answered the test questions, the former scoring 42.6 per cent and the latter 55.6 per cent.

Steele and Aronson (1995) conducted research with African-American Caribbean college students. The test was taken from the Graduate Record Examination and was preceded by a simple pre-test, which collected some basic personal background and which included some details on ethnicity. The mere engagement with these basic questions evoked negative stereotypes, which cut the test scores by half.

These examples graphically illustrate the reduction in performance when negative frames of reference or story influence our thinking. Consider how the performance of school leaders might deteriorate if they are pressed to adopt a negative view of their leadership by Ofsted, a local authority adviser or School Improvement Partner. No leader expects to be cosseted and insulated from challenge. There is, however, a need to explore strategies that ensure that the performance of leaders is enhanced or protected during the feedback process. There are many examples where corrosive feedback has initially damaged leadership performance and subsequently led to dismissal, breakdown or disengagement.

Our adoption of negative stories changes our thinking at a profound level. Our brains are wonderfully sophisticated but their core processes are linked to securing our survival. Imagine for a moment that you are sat on the beach on a warm afternoon, you can hear the sound of the sea and your hand is clutching a glass of chilled Chardonnay. If that is an attractive scenario you would need little encouragement to linger in that situation. If, however, you are confronted by a negative image, for example dealing with a coercive chair of governors with the empathy and compassion of a house brick, you will feel uncomfortable. However, being a consummate professional committed to the achievement of young people (not to mention that you have a mortgage to pay and children to keep in the manner to which you would like to become accustomed) you stand your ground. The survival mechanisms rooted in your emotional brain, the limbic system, will now turn up the volume and sharpen the contrast. Literally what was bad is now portrayed as even worse in an attempt to get you to take action (the operation of this mechanism is explored further in Chapter 4).

One of the key changes that begins to emerge from this state is 'all or nothing' thinking:

> When you are stressed, your brain works differently. You are more likely to resort to 'All or Nothing' thinking, which causes catastrophising and difficulties in solving complex problems. In turn this causes more arousal, or stress and so continues the 'loop' exhausting you. (Elliott and Tyrrell, 2003, page 18)

Most situations that we experience are simply not extreme; there are elements of good and bad in them. A recent holiday in Cyprus was good if you discounted the three days of torrential rain and the fourteen-hour thunderstorm in the middle. Even schools in challenging circumstances have glimmers of hope! When an individual loses this broader and more balanced picture circumstances are viewed through distorting lenses and even language changes. Elliott and Tyrrell (2003) have identified key words that indicate if someone is engaging in this kind of thinking (see Figure 3.1).

Always	Never	Perfect
Impossible	Awful	Terrible
Ruined	Disastrous	Furious

Figure 3.1 Words that indicate 'all or nothing' thinking
Source: Elliott and Tyrrell (2003, page 45)

When we allow our thinking to become distorted in this way situations can rapidly invoke despair. The difficult colleague becomes a 'psychopath' or 'impossible', the budget deficit equates with 'bankruptcy' and the difficult staff meeting becomes 'mutiny'. The list goes on. This is not to trivialize the difficult situations that face school leaders but there must be mechanisms to triangulate our perceptions. Antidotes to this style of thinking will be considered in more detail in the concluding chapter.

Mention has already been made of Alan Flintham's research. The report *Reservoirs of Hope* is based on interviews with 25 serving headteachers drawn from a range of phases and contexts. Alan's focus is on hope arguing that it is this which 'drives the institution forward towards achieving its vision, whilst allowing it to remain true to its values whatever the external pressures' (page 3). He refers back to John West-Burnham (2002), who had talked of leaders needing to have an 'internal personal reservoir of hope', which Flintham extends to be the 'calm centre at the heart of the individual leader from which their values and vision flow and which continues to enable effective interpersonal engagement and sustainability of personal self-belief in the face of not only day to day pressures but critical incidents in the life of the school' (page 3).

I would argue that at the core of the concept of hope is the underpinning positive story, which represents a 'reservoir' both for the leader and to those around. Conversely, a negative story could be equated with the ebbing of hope and it will result in the change in thought patterns along the lines that have been described.

The Good Book

Many senior leaders receive precious few positive comments. It is almost as if those around believe that they have 'grown out' of the need for praise. Leaders, of course, need neither plastic praise nor the acclaim of sycophants but like all human beings they do thrive on positive feedback. It is probable that the carving at the top of the totem pole is in receipt of more bird droppings than those further down. It can certainly feel that way as a senior leader in a school or indeed in other organizations.

A practical strategy is to keep a 'Good Book'. This is a simple personal scrapbook in which you place those letters of thanks, and record those positive comments and incidents from staff and pupils and indeed others. Turning its pages on dark cheerless days that inevitably come in leadership can help restore perspective. Banal? Perhaps it is but then not everything good has to be sophisticated.

Holding your own

Most people like to think that they are fair and open-minded, ready to be convinced by another person's point of view. This is a commendable position but one which is sadly at odds with our day-to-day experience. People seem capable to hold on to viewpoints with incredible tenacity in the face of contradictory information and leaders are no different. Many of us have known for a long time that other people do this; perhaps it is the moment to reflect on our personal aptitude for bias. It may well be that our beliefs and opinions are closely wedded to who we are as people.

Consider two people arguing as to whether they would rather drive a Volkswagen or a Ford. Certainly technical information might come into the discussion: brake horsepower, customer satisfaction surveys, fuel economy and acceleration, etc. The reality is that they are both good cars and yet a comment such as 'I wouldn't be seen dead in [insert the vehicle of choice here]' is not an impressive indicator of cognitive processing.

> Man is not a rational animal, he is a rationalizing animal. (Heinlein, 1953, page 27)

More recently this ability of human beings to defend their particular position or own brand of thinking has been explored by psychologists. Lord et al. (1979) presented evidence supporting or rejecting the effectiveness of capital punishment to a mixed group holding divergent views on the subject (24 advocates and the same number of antagonists). The research team hypothesized that each opposing group would use the same pieces of evidence to further support their opinions. After reading an article on capital punishment the subjects were given detailed research descriptions of the study they had just read but this time it included procedure, results, prominent criticisms and results shown in a table or graph. They were then asked to evaluate the study, stating how well it was conducted and how convincing the evidence was overall.

The results were in line with the researchers' hypothesis; in fact there was even greater polarization of views amongst some participants than had been expected. Students found that studies which supported their pre-existing view were superior to those which contradicted it, in a number of detailed and specific ways. In fact, the studies all described the same experimental procedure but with only the purported result changed. Overall there was a pronounced increase in the polarization of opinion. Initial analysis of the experiment shows that proponents and opponents confessed to shifting their attitudes slightly in the direction of the first study they read. Once subjects read the more detailed study, they returned to their original belief regardless of the evidence provided, pointing to the details that supported their viewpoint and disregarding anything that was to the contrary. This is termed confirmation bias.

Even more intriguing was the study undertaken by Blagov et al. (2006). Functional neuroimaging (fMRI) was used to study a sample of committed Democrats and Republicans during the three months prior to the 2004 US presidential elections. Each group was given the task of considering threatening or contradictory information relating to their candidate of choice, John Kerry or George Bush respectively. During the task the subjects were scanned to see what parts of their brain were active.

The fMRI showed emotional areas of the brain activating but did not see any increased activation of the parts of the brain normally engaged during reasoning. Instead, they saw a network of emotion-based circuits lighting up, including circuits hypothesized to be involved in regulating emotion, and areas linked to resolving conflicts.

Participants returned to their biased conclusions and found ways to discard rational information to sustain their own position. Of course the discrediting information relating to the opposing candidate was gratefully received. Once their preferred bias had been restored the brain rewarded itself with a secretion of dopamine. This would produce a pleasant high and would therefore confirm the 'rightness' of moving back to their original and preferred position.

The inclusion of research into confirmation bias is not about engendering self-doubt or undermining self-confidence. It is about arguing that those in leadership roles should ensure that systems are in place to check their views, policies, vision and perceptions. This is part of the strength of teams and it again justifies the regular interface with a competent mentor coach. The latter can explore and challenge the story that you inhabit. As Shakespeare adroitly observed: 'There is nothing either good or bad, but thinking makes it so' (*Hamlet*, act 2 scene 2).

4 A peace of my mind

It is how people respond to stress that determines whether they will profit from misfortune or be miserable. (Csikszentmihalyi, 1990)

If you are distressed by anything external, the pain is not due to the thing itself, but to your estimate of it; and this you have the power to revoke at any moment. (Marcus Aurelius Antonius)

Case study: Stressed to kill

In my work as a consultant and mentor I visit a wide range of schools. Several months ago I went to discuss the development of a project with a deputy head and was also asked to meet the headteacher. The latter was, and indeed is, highly respected but definitely at the formidable end of the leadership spectrum. She has a leadership style analogous to an icebreaker crossing the Barents Sea.

Discussion of the project was bypassed and forty minutes was given to a diatribe on a problem with a difficult parent. The issue was largely procedural but had spilled over into litigation. At the end of the session she shook her head, apologized for the diversion and we returned to the intended topic.

During the telling of the story her voice was raised in both volume and pitch. There was bodily agitation expressed particularly through hand and then whole arm movements. Eye contact was seldom made; rather, her eyes were scanning around the room as if suspecting an assault on the office were imminent. Inappropriate confidential information was shared with me. The language used was confrontational with frequent use of words such as win, attack and victory.

I was witnessing a serious manifestation of stress affecting body, thinking, judgement and language.

A few years ago I was talking to an acquaintance about his passion for drag racing. He raced a highly tuned large motorbike. This was equipped with a cylinder of nitrous oxide with the gas being injected into the engine at the push of a large red button on the handlebars. Hitting this produced spectacular results with the motorbike flying forwards like 'fertilizer off a spade'. This was both good news and bad news. Certainly, insane levels of acceleration were achieved; the downside was that extended use of this oxygen-rich gas would cause the engine to go into terminal meltdown. The application of this metaphor to the role of leadership is surely self-evident.

Educational leaders tend to fall into two categories. First, there are those for whom a planned approach to stress management would be of general benefit and could improve both performance and indeed their enjoyment of the role itself. The second group needs a more urgent response. They have already hit the 'red button' and are heading towards a potentially catastrophic emotional and even physical meltdown.

Alan Flintham recognized the differing levels of self-awareness in headteachers and identified three groups. The first he designated 'strider' heads. These were leaders who moved on after a successful school experience. This was in accordance with a clear career plan and with a proactive exit strategy and who moved on despite pleas for them to continue. They found a subsequent new context re-energizing. The second group he termed 'stroller' heads. Members of this group began to see the 'writing on the wall' and walked away from headship in a controlled manner. They identified concerns over work–life balance, change, pressures or philosophical issues and took action. A final category of heads, probably those most at risk, were identified as 'stumbler' heads. This group frequently suffered 'burnout' through the failure of their sustainability strategies to cope, which resulted in stress-related or ill-health retirement.

No leader should experience the misery of this level of stress neither should they operate without having a regular personal review of their circumstances, workload and stress. Whilst space for personal reflection can be helpful, the exploration with a competent mentor is even more beneficial. It is highly unlikely that School Improvement Partners will fulfil such a role and the facilitation of such a process by hard-pressed staff of the local authority or by a chair of governors is at the best happenstance. Boyatzis and McKee (2005) speak of a 'cycle of sacrifice and renewal' being at the heart of task of leadership. Mentors are needed who can both support such a review and initiate strategies that take staff forward beyond survival.

In engaging in such a review process there is a need to recognize that we are multidimensional beings. Our brains are not segregated into home, work and leisure. Problems and stress in one area will inevitably spill over into other areas of our lives. Life crises such as death of a spouse, divorce or financial difficulty can disrupt even the best plans and stress management regimes. Different life crises have different impacts. In many cases, however, it may be possible to anticipate crises and prepare for them. It may also be useful to recognize the impact of crises that have occurred so that you can take account of them appropriately.

Interesting work in this area was undertaken by Holmes and Rahe (1967) leading to the development of the Social Readjustment Scale. This allocates a number of Life Change Units (LCUs) to different events, so that you can evaluate them and take action accordingly. This venerable approach is perhaps an oversimplification of complex situations and does not include some more contemporary causes of stress. It can, however, provide a useful baseline in adjusting to life crises. If you have a high score, or know that you will have a high score in the future, it may be worth pre-empting any problems by adopting stress management strategies perhaps by even saying no to demands.

Of course not all stressors are negative. Add together your score for significant life events over the last two years in Figure 4.1 and compare the total with those in Figure 4.2.

Cycling can damage your health

Many occupations have cycles of ebb and flow in workloads. Accountants, for example, tend to come under pressure towards the end of the fiscal year, so do farmers at harvest times and doctors in winter with cold and flu epidemics. Arguably those in education experience the impact of cyclical working in a more extreme way. Teachers and school leaders are enmeshed in a cycle of holiday–term–holiday, etc. Unusually the whole organization follows a cycle of intense activity followed by virtual shutdown; the term starts with high energy and frequently grinds to a conclusion. This is akin to running a marathon and collapsing on the finishing line. School leaders are all too frequently dependent on the end or term and the holiday as a strategy for coping with stress. At senior levels this approach is further undermined by stockpiling 'non-urgent' tasks for the holidays. Many leaders start the holiday with a serious backlog of work to be completed before the start of the next term. During term-time they went home with a bulging briefcase. At the end of term work is taken home by filling the boot of the car with boxes of documents. A further downside from this reliance on holidays as a core 'stress-busting' strategy is that the benefit of these breaks seems to diminish as time goes on. It takes longer to recover in the holidays and the recovery is progressively less beneficial. Consider the graph showing energy levels in holiday periods (Figure 4.3).

One brain, two minds

Frequently indecision has been depicted as the person 'being in two minds'. Perhaps this old adage captures some of the reality of our human predicament. Evolutionary development has left us with two connected but distinctive neurological areas. The interplay

Life events	Score
Death of a spouse	100
Divorce	73
Marital separation from mate	65
Detention in jail, or other institution	63
Death of close family member	63
Major personal injury or illness	53
Marriage	50
Dismissal from work	47
Marital reconciliation	45
Retirement	45
Major change in the health or behaviour of a family member	44
Pregnancy	40
Sexual difficulties	39
Gaining a new family member (through birth or adoption)	39
Major business change (reorganization, merger, bankruptcy)	39
Major change in financial status	38
Death of a close friend	37
Change to a different line of work	36
Major change in the number of arguments with spouse	35
Taking out a mortgage or loan for a major purchase	31
Foreclosure on a mortgage or loan	30
Major change in responsibilities at work	29
Son or daughter leaving home (e.g. marriage or college)	29
Trouble with in-laws	29
Outstanding personal achievement	28
Spouse beginning or ceasing to work outside the home	26
Beginning or ceasing formal schooling	26
Major change in living conditions	25
Revision of personal habits (dress, manners, associations, etc.)	24
Trouble with boss	23
Major change in working hours or conditions	20
Change in residence	20
Change to a new school	20
Major change in usual type and/or amount of recreation	19
Major change in church activities (a lot more or a lot less)	19
Major change in social activities (clubs, dancing, cinema, etc.)	18
Taking out a small loan (e.g. car, freezer, etc.)	17
Major change in sleeping habits	16
Major change in the number of family get-togethers	15
Major change in eating habits	15
Holidays	13
Christmas season	12
Minor violations of the law (e.g. speeding or parking tickets)	11
Total	

Figure 4.1 Life crises and stress

Fewer than 150 Life Change Units	=	30% chance of developing a stress-related illness
150–299 Life Change Units	=	50% chance of illness
Over 300 Life Change Units	=	80% chance of illness

Figure 4.2 Life crises and ill-health

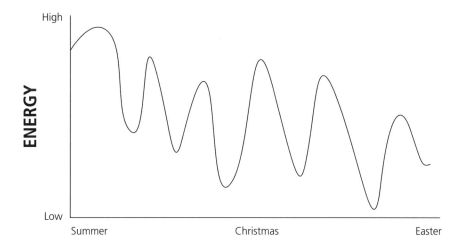

Figure 4.3 Energy and holidays

of these is significant both in generating stress and depression and in its subsequent management. A basic understanding of the neurology and physiology involved can be a significant benefit in understanding stress and its management.

To consider the model of one brain and two minds: the first in view is the cognitive brain, sometimes referred to as the 'headmind'. It is situated in a number of areas of the brain but notably the cerebral cortex. This is the complex covering of the brain and is where working memory is situated, where perception is created and where control over hands, fingers, arms and legs originates. Towards the front of this is the prefrontal cortex, just above the eyes. This is where thinking takes place, activity such as analysis, decision making, creativity, conforming to rules and planning. Either side of the head are the temporal lobes, which are engaged in recognizing speech, assessing visual information and storing factual information about our experience (but crucially not emotional memories); these areas are also the seat of language. The key role of our headmind is to process and interpret information and subsequently decide the best course of action in our interests.

The second area is the 'bodymind', which includes our 'emotional brain' and is, in many ways, more complex. It is an integrated network of parts of the brain, the nervous system, the endocrine system and which even operates at a cellular level. At its core is the limbic system, the midbrain region. This contains the hippocampus, which is where emotional memories are stored and brought out when our cognitive brain explores its archives of factual memories. The fascinating amygdalae, which approximate to the alarm centre of the brain, can override nearly everything else in attempts to secure our survival. The thalamus processes information derived from the senses. There is also the hypothalamus, which is the body's master controller. It regulates sleep, reproductive activity, temperature and even water retention. The hypothalamus is also the root producer of our emotions. Dimensions of the bodymind form the basis of current discussions about emotional intelligence.

In recent years the importance of emotion has been increasingly realized. Daniel Goleman (1996) has both popularized the concept and highlighted its seminal role in leadership. It is routinely explored in leadership courses and programmes such as National Professional Qualification for Headship or Leading from the Middle. I retain some unease as to how emotions can be discussed using a largely cognitive/rational framework.

This sub-cognitive complex which is being aggregated here as 'the bodymind' acts as an 'emotional radar'. Eaton (2006) and Goleman (2006) also describe it as the 'low road'; it can be regarded as 'quick and dirty'. Gladwell (2005) has described some of the functions of our bodymind when it provides us with information, which leaves our headmind trying to work out where the information has come from. He cites the research, in the USA, of Wendy Levinson et al. (1997), which was extended by Nalini Ambady et al. (1997). These researchers recorded hundreds of conversations between doctors and patients. Half of these doctors had never been sued; the other half had been sued for malpractice at least twice. Ambady edited the conversations with 114 of the doctors into 20-second soundbites and then applied acoustic filters to mask the content. These recordings were then played to judges who were asked which of the doctors were most likely to be sued. All the judges had was these 20-second recordings, which preserved rhythm, tonality and pitch but which had no discernable content. The judges' predictions as to whether a particular doctor was likely to be sued or not were uncannily accurate. Professor Ambady recorded that she and her colleagues were 'totally stunned by the results' (page 42).

These findings mirror the experience of many school leaders conducting interviews for posts. Frequently we form strong impressions of our like or dislike of a candidate within seconds of meeting them. The rest of the day is spent using an intricate interviewing procedure with that intuitive conclusion 'nagging' away in the background. Of course this intuition from our bodymind is by no means foolproof; however, many leaders have regretted overriding its advice in the face of skills matrices and 'in-tray exercises'.

Discussions around emotional intelligence seem to focus on its use or the control, containment or management of emotions. It would appear that in many instances the 'emotional brain', centred on the limbic system, seems to be viewed as a 'wildchild'. This is to make a whole series of serious errors. First, as Eaton (2006) notes: 'Bodymind is the intelligence of the body, working through the brain, the nervous system, the glands and the cells and the immune system. Its primary function is to ensure the safety of the individual and to maximize health and happiness' (page 5).

The purpose of our bodymind is to guard, guide and protect. It is a friend, not an embarrassing imbecile locked in the attic. The second serious error is that western society has given excessive value to headmind or cognitive intelligence. This is an arrogant assumption, which reduces our essential humanity. Third, the suppression of bodymind messages is inherently dangerous and at the root of stress and depression and can cause ill-health.

It is unlikely that our brains have changed significantly over the last ten thousand years. Evolution is a painfully slow process. However, the context within which we now use our brains has altered almost beyond recognition. We are using brains which have had fundamentally the same structure, capacity and operating systems for thousands of years for an incredible range of new and challenging tasks.

One of our core survival mechanisms is centred on the so-called hypothalamus–pituitary–adrenal axis. This generates the flight or fight response and most people recognize this as the release of adrenaline and cortisol which puts our body on red alert to meet a threatening situation. The operation of this process is well known, for example that near miss with a car when crossing the road. This mechanism, which enabled survival when confronted by a woolly mammoth, is exactly the same system which engages when we have to work in difficult circumstances or with an undermining senior colleague. The former challenge could last for minutes whilst the latter could last for weeks, months or even years. Of course the arrows that hit us are not usually fired by only a single archer!

Earlier I used John Eaton's term about our limbic system providing an emotional radar. This is a useful metaphor. When the bodymind, through the limbic system, perceives a threat it signals this danger to the headmind. This is where the tension can begin. The headmind is significantly rule-bound; it works on assumptions and its language is word and symbol – all of which are learned from others. The cognitive brain or headmind has developed a sense of how things ought to be, how we should behave and has a huge repertoire of 'disaster movies' that it will play if we are tempted to take a 'non-conventional' course of action. The consequence is that our headmind blocks the bodymind's call for 'action this day'. Your bodymind is telling you that you are in a threatening situation. Your headmind is telling you that you are a professional and should be able to deal with this, like the quote from the head already cited. Escape is not an option because you have responsibilities: a mortgage, family – and what would people think? Actually, thinking like this is already evidence that you are moving into 'all or nothing' thinking, which is a consequence of stress and certainly in turn increases its intensity.

The bodymind or emotional brain makes the message expressed through emotion and feelings more insistent. The headmind responds by churning the thoughts round and round without any real outcomes. It is this churning which disturbs sleep. Unresolved emotional issues are usually worked through during dreaming. If no resolution is reached we actually begin to 'over-dream' in an attempt to clear these emotions (Elliott and Tyrrell, 2003, page 29). This is exhausting and the brain wakes us to escape this draining activity.

Concurrently the adrenaline and cortisol flowing through our bodies for an extended period is affecting our health: typically tiredness, grey appearance as the blood supply to our skin is restricted, agitated movements, inability to concentrate, ill-thought-through decisions, disturbed sleep, changes in appetite and raised blood pressure. It is at this point that stress takes a new turn. The hypothalamus registers that the body is running beyond its normal capacity and employs a strategy to dampen the situation down by reducing the amount of mood enhancing neurotransmitters notably serotonin and norepinephrine. There is now a movement towards depression.

Depression is a complex state which further affects our thinking and our ability to function at many levels. Typically you may:

- feel sad and miserable;
- feel exhausted;
- feel that even small tasks seem to be insurmountable;
- find previously enjoyable activities routine;
- suffer from brain-fog;
- feel that the future offers little that is positive;
- feel angry and irritable;
- lack confidence, perhaps in speaking to others – or even answering the phone or opening letters causes anxiety;
- find sleeping difficult and wake in the early hours;
- feel that there is no way out of a situation;
- believe that others just put up with you and that you are a burden;
- feel that you are a failure or feel guilty that you have let others down;
- spend a lot of time 'churning over' the situation;
- find making decisions difficult.

Stress and depression are serious conditions and should be addressed as priorities. The following actions are well worth exploring:

- Seek the advice of your doctor. It is important to check both general health and conditions resulting from stress such as high blood pressure. Antidepressants may well be prescribed. Elliott and Tyrrell (2003), however, argue that these work for only one-third of those who take them and are only partially effective for a further third. They do not work at all for the remaining third and many people experience unacceptable side effects from these drugs. They are dealing only with symptoms and if the underlying cause is not addressed the subsequent relapse rate is high.

Other avenues of action are important. **It is imperative if you are taking antidepressants that you do not stop taking them or change the dosage without medical advice.**

- Counselling is a very apposite support, particularly if it is based on cognitive behaviour therapy, interpersonal therapy or solution-focused therapies. There is a need to break unhelpful and destructive thinking patterns and explore possibilities and options in the future. Above all else the stressed or depressed person needs to have his or her thinking challenged.

> People who tend towards analysing what has gone wrong in their lives, reviewing the past selectively (picking out the negative aspects), catastrophising every little setback, dreaming up future disasters or engaging in self-blame, tend to stay locked into the state of depression instead of rising above it. This explains something observed for some time – that depressed people habitually adopt a particular way of thinking to explain things that happen to and around them. (Griffin and Tyrrell, 2004, page 249)

Griffin and Tyrrell (2004) also advocate caution in considering psychodynamic counselling. Rooted in Freud's work this seeks to find explanations for repressed past events especially in childhood. A feature of depression is excessive introspection so that an approach based on this is unlikely to be appropriate.

- Attend to issues like a healthy diet and lifestyle; perhaps seek advice on alcohol consumption and smoking if these are issues for you.
- Exercise can be hugely beneficial in 'burning off' adrenaline and producing mood-enhancing natural body chemicals, endorphins. Regular exercise may even fight depression as effectively prescription medication. If, however, you have not exercised regularly it is important to seek medical advice before starting.
- Try to find something that you actually enjoy doing rather than something that you think you ought to enjoy doing.
- Check your workload. Are there areas that you can delegate? Is there a way that you could move to a greater level of shared leadership? If your approach is very hierarchical then this could be explored with a mentor. This could be a reflection of your style or perhaps be imposed on you by the expectations of others. Shared leadership is very much about an atmosphere of trust (see Figure 4.4).

Control	Delegation	Empowerment	Subsidiarity
Low trust			High trust
Immaturity			Maturity
Dependency			Independence

Figure 4.4 Trust and organizational relationships

- Relaxation is good and indeed the opposite to depression is not happiness but calmness. However, it is important not to set up situations that create the context for excessive introspection and 'churning'.

Mihaly Csikszentmihalyi (1990) encouraged reflection on what it is like to be in an optimal state, which he describes as 'flow'. Arguably this concept of flow is about creativity; it is the place where problems are understood as opportunities and where challenge is a growth point rather than a threat. In leadership terms it is the point where the future transcends the present, the place of innovation and dreams. Stress and depression are the enemies of generating change and progress and as such are the cancer of leadership and must not go unresolved.

> Over the endless dark centuries of evolution, the human nervous system has become so complex that it is now able to affect its own states, making it to a certain extent functionally independent of its genetic blueprint and of the objective environment. A person can make himself happy or miserable, regardless of what is actually happening 'outside,' just by changing the contents of consciousness. We all know individuals who can transform hopeless situations into challenges to be overcome, just through the force of their personalities. This ability to persevere despite obstacles and setbacks is the quality people most admire in others, and justly so: it is probably the most important trait for succeeding in life, but for enjoying it as well. (Csikszentmihalyi, 1990, page 24)

5 Values for money

Given the status and authority accorded to leaders, not least in schools, there does seem to be a justification for the expectation that behaviour of leaders will model and exemplify the expectations in the community in the professional context if no other. (West-Burnham, 2003, page 5)

You don't have to be Mother Theresa to have moral purpose. Some people are deeply passionate about improving life (sometimes to a fault, if they lack one or more components of leadership: understanding of the change process, strong relationships, knowledge building and coherence making amongst multiple priorities). Others have a more cognitive approach, displaying less emotion but still being intensely committed to betterment. Whatever one's style, every leader, to be effective must have and work on improving his or her moral purpose. (Michael Fullan, 2001, page 13)

A model for values

So much of our society is described as being 'post-' something, for example Christian, modern, industrial. This period of uncertainty has produced a reduction in moral confidence. Leaders often go so far as to question whether they have a right to hold or express values of their own in a professional context. Certainly values change over time. In the early nineteenth century flogging pupils was widely accepted; around that time the infamous Dr Keate of Eton once flogged the boys sent to him as Confirmation candidates. The mistake occurred because the list of candidates was on the same size piece of paper as the punishment forms. Canings were routinely taking place in state schools within the last twenty years. It is interesting to speculate why views about the appropriateness of this punishment changed. Have the values held in schools altered or is it more about legislation? Probably there are a number of answers; indeed there will be some teachers and politicians who would even welcome its return.

Consider for a moment that you are an advocate of corporal punishment. What would be your justification? Some people might take a pragmatic line and argue that deteriorating behaviour by pupils would benefit from a short sharp shock. However, if you were to reach deeper into your thinking what would such a stance say about your views on the worth and value of individuals, about your understanding about motivation and what sort of future society is such punishment paving the way for? Thinking about moral issues is never simple; it always starts to come apart like layers of an onion.

John West-Burnham has produced a useful model for thinking through morals, values and ethics, by the analogy of a tree (see Figure 5.1).

Morals (the branches) – the choices and decisions which derive from your values

Values (the trunk) – the view of how things should be in a specific time and place. They may vary or be refined, say in a school or a social setting.

Ethics (the roots) – the bedrock of our beliefs about right and wrong and how the world should be. They may be derived from a faith position or philosophy or developed in an ad hoc manner of time

Figure 5.1 A model for morals, values and ethics

Many people have found this diagram of use. In particular it has helped to shed light on the fact that though our values may remain consistent our moral choices will not necessarily remain uniform. Of course we can translate our ethics into a personal value system for use in our school. It is crucial to realize that the school is an organic whole and its value system is a synthesis of the views of a community. Significant problems can occur when such a community simply assumes that its values are understood, when values remain implicit rather than being made explicit.

Nothing is straightforward. Consider the following scenario.

Your school is close to capacity; there is just one place left before appeals will be required. On the Monday a family visits the school wanting a place for their son. He is a Year 8 pupil who has not settled in his previous school. Apparently he has learning difficulties, which may be along the Asperger's line, and there is some talk of a statement. The family have moved into the area and seem supportive. They are informed that a decision will be made following contact with the boy's previous school.

On the Tuesday a second family are interviewed; again they have just moved into the area. They have a daughter. Reports are produced which show the girl to be able across a wide range of subjects. She is also very musical and in her previous school was on the school council. The parents mention that they had been heavily involved in the school association of the previous school. What would be your decision?

In a smaller school the admission of the second pupil, the girl in preference to the boy with learning difficulties, could mean the difference of a 2 per cent increase in the 5-plus A*–C category in three years' time. Demands on staff would also be reduced and it is likely that a raft of problems would be avoided. The school's mission statement is 'Achievement for All' – how would that sit with the rejection of the boy? The time for developing both individual educational values and those of the school is before tackling decisions like this. Ad hoc decisions taken only on pragmatic grounds begin to accumulate and to shape the organization in a random manner. It will also have an impact on the development of shared leadership because there is little commonality of purpose and direction.

All decisions have a moral basis whether they are about staffing, discipline, budget or the curriculum. A range of different outcomes can still be consistent with an established value system. The value system itself does not have a self-evident claim to be accepted as a moral imperative. It too must have sound foundations within an ethical framework. Consider the following case study.

Case study: Tunnel vision

At a professional development day for headteachers James began to share his approach to leading his school. The school had gone through a long period of average to below-average performance. This mediocrity was challenged by an Ofsted Inspection. James reformulated his educational value system in very finite terms. He stated it as being about a particular level of performance at KS3 and particular achievement levels at the end of KS4 in terms of 5-plus A*–C grades. He was prompted to expand on his principles and vehemently replied that the ones that he had given were all that there were.

In the conversation that followed it became clear that he was wholly consistent in using these 'values' as the benchmark for his direction and actions. Staffrooms were removed at a stroke, as were duties and cover. There was a supervision team run by the catering manager, who managed the children 'in a way that teachers would not be able to do'. Disruptive pupils were simply sent home without appropriate procedures being followed. Intriguingly most of the leadership team were large men; in fact they looked like the Pontypridd front row. They all carried radios and emerged like the flying squad when summoned to the scene of any disturbance.

I found the conversation rather worrying. My misgivings were given legs when talking to one of his staff. When James had this 'Road to Damascus' experience one of his first steps was to put pressure on his senior leadership team. At least one had a nervous breakdown and another returned to mainstream teaching. It was not unknown for staff that fell out of favour to find photocopies of potential jobs in their pigeon-holes extracted from the *Times Educational Supplement*.

Of course James witnessed a rise in student performance, which was largely applauded by parents.

It cannot be denied that James operated in total harmony with his value system but many would not like such a coercive approach. It was very much a case of the end justifying the means. The problem, I would suggest, is that the value system has not flowed out of a mature and reflective ethical understanding. James was totally sincere; however, sincerity must remain one of the most overrated virtues.

Several years ago I was invited to work with the staff of a Church of England primary school to establish agreed core values. Shifts in the population had resulted in a significant number of both pupils and staff coming from an Islamic background. The task was to find common ground without losing the faith identity of the school and not simply agreeing a consensus, which had no strength and which would frustrate all parties. We started the process by listening to the passions that the staff had for the education of children and to their vision of working in this particular educational community. From this were developed 'Five Cornerstones':

1. spiritual security
2. forgiveness
3. integrity
4. individual worth
5. hope.

In many ways that was the easy part; the challenging task was translating these into policy protocol, curriculum, pedagogy and professional relationships. To have any worth values must become all-pervasive. The talk must be walked, failure is acceptable; however, dissent is not.

The consistent leader

In many ways this should be seen as an aspiration rather than an actuality: 'This is not to argue that every leader should be a paragon but rather their actions should be seen to be ethically based, value driven and morally consistent' (West-Burnham, 2003, page 5).

Southworth (2004) has developed a leadership model that seeks to place a definitive stamp on educational leadership. He argues that leaders can influence what happens in classroom by modelling, monitoring and engaging in dialogue about learning and teaching (see Figure 5.2).

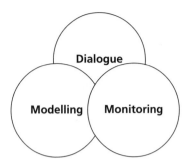

Figure 5.2 Strategies for learning-centred leadership (after Southworth, 2004)

In the context of this chapter it is the modelling dimension of the model that is central. Southworth defines modelling as:

Modelling is concerned with the power of example. Teachers and headteachers believe in setting an example because they know this influences pupils and colleagues alike. Research shows that teachers watch their leaders closely. And teachers watch what their leaders do in order to check if the leaders' actions are consistent over time and to test whether leaders do as they say. Teachers do not follow leaders who cannot 'walk the talk'. (page 6)

Tim Brighouse (2003) posed the following questions to stimulate thinking about how well values are rooted in practice:

- Do we assess the child's preferred learning style and intelligence or talent profile on entry? How does that inform our teaching styles and organisation of learning?
- Do we have at least two timetables for the pupils, one reflecting the wish to proceed simultaneously across a broad balanced curriculum, the other offering immersion opportunities to accelerate learning according to the learner's interest or need?
- How do timetables vary for different year groups and how do they compare with the practice of other schools?
- Do we encourage competition among pupils in settled groups and avoid it in mixed-ability groups?
- How does that vary for whole-class competition? Does our competition policy allow everyone engaged in it to win, albeit at different speeds?
- How is emphasis given to ipsative competition?
- Does our library stock/resource reflect people (achievements or failures) of different ethnicity, gender, race and ability?
- Who took part in the review and consequential purchase of stock –development/management team, whole staff, parents, pupils?
- Do we know the names of those children in public care in our school?
- What is their attendance and performance? How is it improving over time?

- Do we ensure that poverty is not a barrier to children on free school meals in accessing the curriculum (e.g. materials, trips)?
- What is the trend in performance (achievement/attendance/attainment) of those eligible for free school meals?
- Do we run ski trips and if we do, who goes on them?
- Do we each year (and is there a calendar?) for every year group have assemblies to illustrate respect, tolerance and achievement of people from different gender, race, religion and ability groups?
- How do we vary it from year to year?
- Do we celebrate the achievements of learners in our community on the same basis of monitoring for balance?
- Does this year affect award or reward systems?
- Do we allocate resources on the basis of differentiated children's needs rather than the same share for all?
- How do we provide extra and focused time for individual pupils known to be at risk, e.g. Muppet-type clubs, other extra-curricular clubs and societies, tutoring, mentoring?
- How do we 'tariff' the code of practice in our schools and how does it compare with other schools?
- Who are the children who do not have a meaningful or special relationship with a teacher or learning assistant in the school community?
- Do we have targets for each individual staff member for actions in the next year which will push our 'inclusive' practice further?
- How are we extending our collective knowledge of the small actions that help daily practice encouraging inclusion?
- Do our published targets for improved attainments help an inclusive climate (i.e. 5 per cent or more A–C or A–E or points per pupil)?
- How do we encourage the home and community curriculum to be inclusive not exclusive? How are the achievements of youngsters outside school (supplementary schools, children's university, hobbies, family trips) celebrated inside school? (pages 3–4)

What would you resign over?

This is an extreme question. Apart from promotion or other such positive reasons for leaving a school, the reality is that most people resign from a post in a negative situation because of relationship issues rather than issues of conscience. Of course such issues can reflect a dissonance between stated values and daily reality.

> ## Case study: Close call
>
> Geraldine is the headteacher of a secondary school in challenging circumstances. The headline of the development plan is raising pupil achievement. The school had struggled for some years to break through a fairly low 'glass ceiling' of results at every level.
>
> Many strategies had been employed including out-of-hours clubs, online homework, a programme of lesson observation and staff mentoring and coaching. It was with some interest that she responded to the chair of governors request that they meet to discuss an idea that he had for raising achievement.
>
> His preamble was to point out that the school had an intake that came from some socially disadvantaged areas. Many of these students were not significantly supported at home. So far so good; Geraldine took some reassurance from being on familiar territory. The chair continued that it was recognized that the school had worked well with youngsters who had special educational needs, indeed that the current school population consisted of some 40 per cent of this type of pupil. Further, he had noted that when exclusion panels were held, it was often these pupils who were featured.
>
> Suddenly the 'big idea' was unveiled. Geraldine should block the admissions of such pupils. He recognized that this was not going to work in every case but a less pleasant and accommodating approach would deter some and prevarication would certainly work with others. He went on to point out that a number of other local heads did this sort of thing to great effect.
>
> Geraldine was stunned. Leaving aside the legislative issues, this flew in the face of everything she had based the development of the school and her own professional values on. One of the school's central values was inclusion.
>
> She went home that evening and concluded that this was a step too far. It was several days before she saw her chair of governors again. In his usual style he had moved on to another topic, this time the storage of Ritalin.
>
> Geraldine had been prepared to resign. It had been a close call.

Leading involves compromise; sometimes it is the melding of your views with those of the team or it may be about implementing government initiatives.

It is important to realize that all compromise carries a cost. It is about auditing that cost carefully and ensuring that the cost does not propel you towards the stress of moral deficit.

Integrity

The domain of values takes us into the area of spiritual leadership. This should not be seen in a narrow religious sense but embracing a broader concept of 'secular spirituality'. In Flintham (2003b) all the headteachers he interviewed indicated that they felt they had a strong moral or spiritual underpinning to their work, if not a specifically religious one. He recorded the following pithy comment from one male secondary head: 'If this had been about religious spirituality, it would have been the shortest interview on record' (page 7). There was a strong feeling about the value of the topic in the way it was being defined. As one female secondary head from a self-declared secular perspective put it: 'The spiritual side of education is the important side . . . it embraces all backgrounds and all faiths' (page 7).

What is under review is the essential integrity or wholeness of who we are and a failure to engage with this results in personal fragmentation. Flintham (2003b) concluded that the spiritual and moral bases of headship described by those interviewed fell into a variety of categories, though many felt that they derived their spirituality from more than one of these:

- *The generational imperative* – where the engagement with leadership draws heavily from our background; for example, one head commented: 'My working class background laid down my core values of inclusivity' (page 7). Another drew vision from politics and making a difference in life: 'I came from a politically active family . . . I was the first from that (working class) family to reach higher education. That's given me a sense of duty to give something back, to make a difference, like it made a difference to me' (page 7).
- *The Christian imperative* – 15 of his sample of 25 cited a Christian value framework as influencing their professional practice. This number is almost double the number of church schools in the sample. Some heads with a Christian value system in non-church schools see themselves as: 'Every decision has to stand the test of comparison against your (publicly avowed) Christian principles' (page 8).
- *The egalitarian imperative* – this centred on a belief in 'the essential goodness of humanity' and the consequent responsibilities that flow from that belief in terms of social justice, social inclusion and equality of opportunity. 'Everyone has the potential to lead a good life . . . the school's job is to realise that potential' (page 8).
- *The vocational imperative* – a number of heads saw their work as a vocation rather than as simply being a job: 'I have a sense of doing the job I'm supposed to be doing' (page 8).
- *The 'transference' imperative* – two heads from more socially advantaged areas cited as their underlying principle that of 'do as you would be done by' and asserted that their decisions were constantly tested against the template of 'Would I be happy if this were happening to my own children?'

Each of these represents a spiritual core to leadership, in some more developed than in others. Taylor (1991) spoke of the concept of ethical authenticity:

> There is a certain way of being that is *my* way. I am called upon to live my life in this way, and not in imitation of anyone else's. But this gives a new importance to being true to myself. If I am not, I miss the point of my life; I miss what being human is for me.
>
> Being true to myself means being true to my own originality, and that is something only I can articulate and discover. In articulating it, I am also defining myself. (page 29)

6 It's only words

If you're choking in a restaurant you can just say the magic words, 'Heimlich manoeuvre', and all will be well. Trouble is, it's difficult to say 'Heimlich manoeuvre' when you're choking to death. (Eddie Izzard)

Sticks and stones may break my bones but words will never hurt me. (G.F. Northall, 1894, *Folk Phrases of Four Counties*)

Much of human experience is interpreted using words. Sometimes our use of words anticipates what is coming (though often incorrectly) and sometimes we use them as story to reconfigure what has happened. Some of this process has been explored in Chapter 3. In this chapter it is our inner dialogue that is under review.

Life sentence

From an early age we have spent many hours combining words to make sentences. This can be a complex process as the simple subject–object–verb becomes elaborated with clauses and tense. What is often missed is the coding that individual words have and their power to carry messages independently of the meaning of the sentence. These are so-called implicit associations.

Srull and Wyer (1979) devised the following scrambled letter test. (I wonder if he devised the dialogue for Yoda as well?)

1. him was worried she always
2. from are Florida oranges temperature
3. ball the throw toss silently
3. she give replace old the
4. he observes occasionally people watches
5. he will sweat lonely they

6. sky the seamless grey is

7. should now withdraw forgetful; we

8. us bingo sing play let

9. sunlight makes temperature wrinkle raisins

Participants in the test were asked to form grammatical four-word sentences from these as quickly as possible. Intriguingly at the end of the exercise the people who took the test walked more slowly and with a stooped posture. They adopted an elderly stance. This was as a result of words embedded in the sentences, for example 'worried', 'old', 'lonely', 'grey' and even 'bingo'.

In the previously considered work by Steele and Aronson (1995) it was key words in a pre-test questionnaire which included giving information on ethnic origin that changed outcomes. The performance of African-Americans fell substantially because even they had imbibed negative stereotypes and these had been brought to the fore by words in the simple question on racial origin.

Bandler and Grinder began to formulate Neuro-Linguistic Programming from their studies of the gestalt psychologist Fritz Perls, the family therapist Virginia Satir and the psychiatrist Milton Erikson. The last utilized embedded messages as a major part of his therapeutic approach. The story is told of his conversations with a terminally ill cancer patient who was in great pain. He irritated the man by talking about growing vegetables. It was only after Erikson had gone that he realized that the pain had gone. In this apparently trivial conversation words had been embedded and subtly emphasized that reduced the construct of the patient's pain.

What pink elephant?

You have probably come across this illustration or one similar. You are told at all costs not to think about 'pink elephants' and of course despite the instruction you visualize a herd of them. Our thinking process is not constrained by the whole sentence but can focus on parts. Frequently in conversations people make comments such as 'Don't worry', 'Don't think about it' or 'That's not a problem'. A similar process to that which occurred with the elephants takes place. The core of the problem is that our brains simply do not know how to handle negatives as a positive. In order to know what not to think of, our brains have first to think of it.

Leaders, managers, teachers and even parents who are trying to help us in the right direction frequently frame the advice as the negative opposite. The consequence is that they inadvertently draw our attention in exactly the direction that they did not want us to take. Aficionados of the classic TV series *Dad's Army* will know Corporal Jones' catchphrase 'Don't panic!' The phrases that we use in this way are legion:

- 'I am not being judgemental.'
- 'I am not being critical.'
- 'It's not that you are being stupid.'
- 'The situation is not desperate.'
- 'It could be worse.'

If you are cycling down a narrow path and there is a concrete block in the middle, you focus on the gap and not the block. Communication is more powerful when desirable behaviours are described rather than spending time describing those that are not wanted. Incorporating this approach in your communications will be hugely powerful. If negative information has to be delivered then end your message with a forward motivational statement, even to yourself.

Ambiguous language does not help in conveying messages. In the previous paragraph was the assertion 'Incorporating this approach in your communications *will* be hugely powerful'. Reflect for a moment on the impact of this sentence if it was changed to 'Incorporating this approach in your communications *could/might/can/should* be hugely powerful'. This is not about slick techniques or an approach which owes more to retail sales. This previous sentence was very deliberately used, it again describes negatives. Many readers would not have thought about it being 'slick', which is a word carrying a lot of baggage, or indeed about 'retail sales'. Effective leaders use language with authentic precision. Understanding our use of language is like catching sight of ourselves in a mirror or a window.

Voices in my head

The good news is that we all hear these voices. Our heads are usually filled with an inner dialogue or self-talk. This self-talk is both an expression of our self-belief and in turn it also shapes what we believe about ourselves and how we will act. The self-talk can of course be positive or self-limiting.

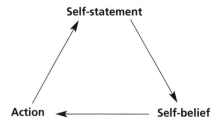

Figure 6.1 The cycle of statement, belief and action

If we are working from a self-limiting belief or set of such beliefs then these can all too frequently become self-fulfilling prophecies in their own right and will dominate our self-talk. Think for a moment about a parachute jump. For some the idea feels exhilarating and exciting whilst for others this is fairly high on their list of things to avoid at all costs. There is of course no reason to voluntarily jump out of a plane with a parachute so the chances are you will not do it. However, many things that we do as leaders are unavoidable. Consider, for example, confronting behaviours, making people redundant, changing the curriculum so that someone's cherished project is axed or excluding that student who regrettably has a parent who is a solicitor. Approaching such situations with a belief that the situation will go wrong will almost certainly secure that outcome. The novelist Richard Bach said, 'Argue for your limitations, and sure enough they're yours'. When the disaster occurs that we believed would happen we have underscored, highlighted and capitalized our original premise and in turn have now reinforced our negative self-belief.

One of the most powerful influences on our attitudes and personalities is what we say to ourselves. It is not what happens to us but how we frame our thoughts around the event. By taking control of this inner dialogue, or 'self-talk', we can begin to assert control over every part of our life.

The words that we use to describe what is happening to us and how we feel about external events will trigger emotions of happiness or unhappiness. When we see things positively and look for good outcomes in every situation and in each relationship, that positive and optimistic approach will become a driver for change. We are constantly faced with challenges, difficulties and problems in life. They are unavoidable and one of the inevitable parts of being human; we can develop resources to respond effectively to each challenge, and in turn become stronger people.

Much of our ability to succeed comes from the way we deal with life. Having a positive mental attitude is indispensable for success and happiness. It is also a key to success as a leader, and it is vital to building strong relationships. Everyone wants to be around a positive person with a cheerful attitude towards life. Few want to be around a negative person who is pessimistic. The ability to develop and maintain a positive mental attitude independent of circumstances will play a critical role in any success that we achieve.

One of the common characteristics of all high-achieving leaders is that they recognize the inevitability of temporary setbacks and disappointments. They accept them as a normal and natural part of their life and role. They do everything possible to avoid problems, but when these come up, successful leaders learn from them and transcend them and continue to move forward towards their goals.

Optimistic people develop the habit of talking to themselves in constructive ways. Whenever they experience adversity of any kind, they immediately describe it to themselves in such a way that it loses its ability to trigger negative emotions. They are able to exert a sense of control by how they describe any event or situation to themselves. In 1879

Thomas Edison (whose entire school experience lasted three months) decided to create a cheap form of lighting using electricity. He was convinced that it was possible but was uncertain how he would achieve this. It took over two thousand trials to finally invent the light bulb. He was asked how he had managed to keep going in the face of so many disappointments and wrong turnings. When he failed he allegedly said, 'I did not see it as a failure, I saw it as a result; I'd just successfully discovered another way not make the light bulb.'

There is a natural tendency in all of us to react emotionally when our expectations are frustrated. When something we wanted and hoped for fails to materialize, we feel a temporary sense of disappointment and unhappiness and possibly disillusionment. A person who is positive and optimistic is resilient and bounces back fast when a setback is encountered. It is perceived as temporary and external. There is a need to take control of the dialogue and counter negative feelings by reframing the event so that appears positive in some way.

Our minds can hold only one thought at a time, either positive or negative; if we deliberately choose the positive thought to dwell upon, our minds are kept in an optimistic frame and negative thoughts are excluded. Since our thoughts and feelings determine our actions, if we keep our words and thoughts framed in a positive manner, we will automatically take a more positive line and move more rapidly towards our intended goals.

It really comes down to the way we talk to ourselves on a daily basis. When a problem or difficulty comes up we must learn to change our language from negative to positive. Earlier we started to explore the concept of problem solving. It is better still to substitute the word 'situation' for 'problem'. Problems are things that we wrestle and struggle with and which carry the force of potential loss and difficultly. A situation, on the other hand, is just something that we deal with. The event is the same but the way we frame the event to ourselves is what makes it sound and appear completely different. An even better word to substitute for the word 'problem' is the word 'challenge'. When we are faced with a difficulty of any kind, instead of saying, 'I have a problem', it is better if we say, 'I have an interesting challenge facing me'. The word challenge is inherently positive. It is again the same situation, only the word that we are using to describe it is different. The situation is moving from threat to opportunity. As a result, our emotional response will also be different.

Affirmations

One powerful way of tackling our self-limiting beliefs is using affirmations. This is a simple tool which works extremely well if it is constructed according to the following protocol.

Crucially, define the behaviour you want or want to change. It could be related to confidence, temper, listening, assertiveness or even more personal issues like weight or drinking. It is essential to frame the affirmation as a positive; it is about achievement rather than avoidance. The following will secure the success of using an affirmation.

- *Personal* – frame the affirmation in the first person singular, I. The desired change will come about because of your own inner picture, which will change as a result of your affirmation.
- *Positive* – where you want to reach must be a positive direction. An affirmation, for example, would not be about controlling temper but about achieving calmness. It would not be about avoiding indecision but about being decisive.
- *Present tense* – affirmations are always written as if they are happening now. The present is actually the only place we inhabit.
- *Definite* – use phrases such as 'I am', 'I do' or 'I have'. Phrases to be avoided are ones which are either conditional such as 'can', 'might' or 'could' or phrases that derive from imposed conventions or expectations, for example 'should' or 'ought', 'need' or 'must'.
- *Written* – as with all intentional behaviour, writing down your targets significantly strengthens the likelihood of outcomes being achieved.
- *Action words* – include words which strengthen the affirmation such as 'confidently', 'energetically or 'with determination'.
- *Visualization* – like the parachute jump, if you cannot see yourself doing something then you will not do it. The picture should be sharp; there is a difference between 'I am enthusiastically learning how to lead in a school' and 'I am enjoying studying for my NPQH'.

The affirmations that you write are yours and are probably best shared sparingly with others and only when you are confident of their support. Review your affirmations as often as possible each day, try for perhaps six sessions. They are not magic incantations; they are about programming your mind. Just reading them has limited impact; however, add to this what it will look like when it is achieved, what you will be thinking and saying at the time and crucially step into the feelings that you anticipate having when your goal is a concrete reality.

A number of the insights on the power of words have been drawn from Neuro-Linguistic Programming (NLP). At one time this was viewed by some in the educational field as a 'dark art'. In recent years it has moved much more into the mainstream of leadership thinking. NCSL now require an understanding of aspects of NLP for facilitators working on the Leading from the Middle programme. The following case study is presented as an example of how powerful and apposite NLP can be.

Case study: circle of excellence

Rebecca had stepped into the breach after the previous headteacher had moved to a post in a larger school. She found herself unexpectedly as the acting head of a 250-pupil primary school. She felt that she was making a good job of leading the school and was giving serious thought to applying for the post on a permanent basis. ⇨

The major difficulty she was experiencing was relating to the governing body. As individuals they were pleasant but given to being patronizing. This approach left Rebecca feeling nervous and not expressing herself clearly at the main governing body meetings. The anticipation of these meetings was escalating out of reasonable proportion.

In a mentoring session we discussed this at length. It was clear that competence was not the issue but rather the situation centred on confidence. I suggested that a classic NLP technique was used to resolve this. What could you accomplish if you had more confidence when you wanted it? Which positive feelings from your past would you want to re-experience if you could transfer them from where they happened in your life to where you really wanted them? The circle of excellence will do just that.

- *Relive confidence.* Stand up and let yourself go back in your memory to a time when you were very confident, abundantly confident. Relive that moment, seeing what you saw and hearing what you heard.
- *Circle of excellence.* As you feel the confidence building in you, imagine a coloured circle on the floor around your feet. Would you like it also to have a sound like a soft hum that indicates how powerful it is? When that feeling of confidence is fullest, step out of that circle, leaving those confident feelings inside the circle. This is an unusual request and you can do it.
- *Selecting cues.* Now think of a specific time in your future when you want to have that same feeling of confidence. See and hear what will be there just *before* you want to feel confident. The cue could be your boss's office door, your office phone or hearing yourself being introduced before a speech.
- *Linking.* As soon as those cues are clear in your mind, step back into the circle and feel those confident feelings again. Imagine that situation unfolding around you in the future with these confident feelings fully available to you.
- *Check the results.* Now step out of the circle again, leaving those confident feelings there in the circle. Outside the circle, take a moment and think again of the forthcoming event. You will find you will automatically recall those confident feelings. This means you have already programmed yourself for that upcoming event. You are feeling better about it and it has not even happened yet. When it arrives, you will find yourself naturally responding more confidently.

Rebecca was initially sceptical but agreed to try out the process. We worked a week before the next full governors' meeting. She was astonished by the difference in her performance; she spoke clearly, marshalling both arguments and facts with alacrity. At one point Rebecca was challenged over a Health and Safety issue related to school visits, and corrected the governor in a pleasant but assertive manner.

She received a lot of positive feedback after the meeting. Several governors commented on the quality of her performance and contrasted it with her earlier input. Of particular note was the fact that Rebecca herself felt that the meeting had gone well and that she felt good in herself.

7 Time will tell

The test of a first-rate intelligence is the ability to hold two opposed ideas in the mind at the same time, and still retain the ability to function. (F. Scott Fitzgerald, *The Crack-Up*, 1936)

Oozing confidence and deliciously spicy, Siena just stepped off the catwalk. This personal organiser has a fashionably soft, relaxed construction, with premium internal features and luxury cream organiser stationery. Width 115mm, height 145mm. (Filofax advert, accessed 1/8/2007)

Juggling jelly

This activity was sadly omitted from NPQH courses but describes the experience of managing time and workflow for many senior leaders! The organization of our time is surprisingly complex. In the first part of the chapter some of the principles will be explored whilst the second part concentrates on practical strategies.

In the past decade the use of IT has become routine, even all-pervasive, and has merited a chapter to itself (Chapter 8). The following case study is extreme and is drawn from real life.

Case study: Chaos theory

Anthea is a whirlwind who swirls into school at eight and seldom leaves before seven in the evening. She has been a deputy for five years and has key responsibilities for finance, budget and human resources. Her office would be a recycler's paradise. Every horizontal surface is covered with 'stacks' – piles of paper which could be categorized only as miscellaneous.

The filing trays have long since lost their separate identities. Intriguingly the filing cabinet has a well-arranged top drawer but three lower drawers which are serving as cupboards. Central to the room is the desk. This has a small central area on which is the computer and a desk diary, several pens and two coffee cups. On the floor are three bags: one for the laptop, a large portmanteau briefcase and a Sainsbury's shopping bag filled with books to be marked.

The owner of the office teaches a half-timetable and flies between lessons meetings, appointments and tasks. Frequently she arrives late at meetings either without papers or hastily reading them in the initial discussions. Many lessons start with an apology to pupils for the fact that a project or essay is not marked.

Today has been particularly stressful. She has put aside two 'free' lessons to complete the FMSiS. This has proved to be wishful thinking, as she has had to sort out a particularly nasty disagreement between two pupils, which included cyber-bullying, and the theft of the victim's iPod. On the way into school she suddenly remembered that it is the first of the month and her car tax expired the day before and she cannot remember exactly where the insurance and MOT certificate is. Do they still allow fourteen days' grace?

It is extremely unlikely that you will hear any leader advocating disorganization and suggesting that chaos is liberating. Most will understand its weight at a pragmatic level; there is a need to go to meetings at the right time and location, a need to meet deadlines, for forward planning in general and, essentially, for specific projects in particular, and procedures for prioritization are sound practice. There is a further imperative for effective time management that is frequently felt but infrequently expressed. Our brains are a phenomenal creative tool working poorly as a neurological office. Using our brains to remember routine things is like Rembrandt putting post-it notes on his painting of *The Return of the Prodigal Son* whilst he was painting it.

Every issue, piece of information and appointment that we are trying to carry in our heads is an 'open-loop'. The brain has to keep it running in case it is forgotten. Stress will result because we have a fear that a vital fact will be forgotten and an important action not taken. Of course the brain has a huge capacity but even so the more we can park 'the routine' the greater will be our relaxation and in turn the greater will be our creative mental energy. This is self-evident: simply try remembering a mental shopping list whilst planning your week's activities at the same time. An effective time management system takes the routine out of the cognitive frame. In the case study Anthea had lots of piles of papers. Imagine the scene if a cleaner descended and restacked them. The resultant stress would be palpable. Anthea is likely to know what is in the piles, at least roughly. This feat is achieved by keeping mental inventories. These have to be kept running and in turn contribute to tiredness and stress.

There are certainly colleagues like the one in the cameo above. The problem is unlikely to be solved with a teacher's planner or a Personal Digital Assistant (PDA). In fact unless some fundamentals are addressed the impositions of such systems are likely to make things worse by creating guilt that the owner is not keeping up with the technology.

Possibly the best starting point is to understand how we work in this context and our personal styles. In Chapter 1 Maccoby's work on personality and leadership was considered; the types reinterpreted here are those who tend to be more interested in detail, those who tend to be more interested in people, and the visionaries. The individuals with the eye for detail and order are likely to have a system in place anyway; they have probably even catalogued their CD collection. It is where the other two types of personality are in the ascendant that problems are more likely to occur. People-centred leaders will tend to drop everything to engage with staff and students. Where the task stopped is probably where it will stay for some time. Visionaries are likely to avoid detail as new ideas tend to eclipse old ones. They simply find detail and completion an anathema. Recognizing your starting point is hugely helpful. The detail-focused person will have to recognize that systems are servants and that the world is a messy place. Sometimes securing the detail may not be the most apposite task for the leader. Leaders in the other two categories will benefit from using planning and organizational systems but will have to overhaul them time and time again.

There are, I would suggest, at least six overarching principles that are needed to underpin the development of time management systems:

1. *The work task of educational leadership is non-linear.* It is a web of tasks. The leader switches from one to other on a frequent basis and is often interrupted as well. Contrast this with a craftsman making a chest of drawers; there is a starting point, middle and conclusion. The sequence that is employed is likely to be the same when he makes the next one. Many time management courses are based on the assumption that work is linear; setting tasks into timeslots throughout the day is frequently at their heart. These are usually small in size in order to fit the size of task to the time available and so reduce 'downtime'. A good time management system must not fall apart every time circumstances change.

2. *Time management should be holistic.* We find it convenient to divide our activities into different areas: home, family, work and leisure, etc. Such segments are not recognized in terms of how the brain works. In the case study above, professional activity was intermingled with personal issues such as taxing the car. It is unrealistic to maintain several systems to organize activity. An integrated approach is likely to keep stress levels to a minimum and also reduce the chances of these different areas coming into conflict.

3. *The system must be reliable.* If our system is patently unreliable we will not trust it. As a consequence the brain will step in to provide a 'belt and braces' back-up system. As soon as this happens we are setting loops running and mitigating the whole process of parking 'to do' activities and information and reducing the capacity of the brain to engage in leadership.

4. *Information and activity.* These are two different areas. It is imperative that we know where to find information from the web, files, documents, etc. Forthcoming activities such as

appointments need to be clearly identifiable. If the two are merged there is an increased risk of confusion and missed appointments because the entry was buried in your diary under the notes from another meeting.

5. *Time is a core leadership skill.* There is little available evidence on how many senior leaders have undertaken training in time management. Anecdotal evidence suggests that very few have done so and that the experience has been variable. Developing expertise in this area is essential for effective performance and also as a means to significantly reduce stress. It should never be viewed as a 'bolt-on'.

6. *It is very much a journey and not a destination.* Time management is an active process which can never be sorted out by completing a course. It is germane to what we undertake as leaders and should be budgeted into our daily and weekly schedules.

Developing a time management system

Various tools and approaches are considered here. All have been proved to work but not all will suit everybody. They are not intended to be prescriptive. You may well find that your own system works better for you. It is, however, worth checking your approach against the six principles outlined in the previous section.

Information and communication systems

It is now very difficult to envisage a working environment without IT; there is a need to address its use, management and impact (the focus of Chapter 8). Many of the tools and systems discussed below have IT-based cousins and these will be considered as alternatives.

Diary

The suggestion here is to restrict information entered in diaries to appointments, times and venues for meetings, and to keep further information, notes, etc. elsewhere. Papers and agendas are best not put in diaries because they make instant access to pages difficult. The diary is the 'one stop shop' for action.

My preference is an A4 diary running through the academic year and then transferred with one for the calendar year. This prevents future events having to be entered in those absurdly small grids at the back. A4 size is harder to lose. It is an obvious point but inserting a return address and a commitment to pay postage for its return is also a practical plus.

The point of contention here is whether to utilize a hard copy, paper format or morph to a PDA. To a large extent this is a matter of personal choice. The electronic form can synchronize with your desktop computer and even that of your secretary. You may want to consider, however, that as a whole-life approach is being advocated here, arguably you may wish not to share more personal details. There are three contraindications which should be given serious consideration:

1. They can lose their charge, which is fated to happen at the most critical moment and of course like other high-tech devices they have been known to crash and even fail completely. The latter is not of course a problem if you have backed up the data!

2. PDAs and electronic diaries do take some time to master. For some people learning the new features and transferring data is a source of deep joy. There are many others for whom the need for IT support is the only justification that they can see for persuading their older teenage children to stay at home, and they are still listening to the wireless and complaining about the scratches on their LPs, proud of that fact that they once sent a text. Probably a PDA is not for them.

3. Data entry – you do need to be able to type at a reasonable rate for this type of technology to be beneficial. Less than around twenty words a minute is too slow. You must also be able to see the text – juggling your PDA and reading glasses at the same time can sometimes appear undignified. Sometimes the term 'senior leader' is not just about role.

Many organizations have committed to using some form of integrated online diary perhaps based on Outlook. In a school context this may be a means of synchronizing the senior leadership team. The implementation of such a system needs commitment from each member of the team and appropriate training together with a coordinator. Whilst for some organizations or teams this is part of their routine for others it has failed after a few days or weeks. The choice is yours but it should not be driven by a strong sense of 'ought'.

Planner

The options in this area are many and can range from the stylish, as in the quote at the beginning of the chapter, to the functional. In general, commercial systems are wedded to a particular method of organization, which may or may not appeal to you as the user. Again the IT alternative is available though the same caveats outlined in the diary section apply. Another possibility is to design your own. The following has been used successfully by a number of leaders. It is cheap, functional and makes a sort of anti-hero type of statement when those with aardvark skin, 16-ring personal organizers surround you.

The core is an A4 ring binder, a pile of A4 paper and a set of dividers. The clever part is that the sections are based around context-specific activities, for example 'at the computer' or 'at school'. The simple 'to do' list is less helpful when it contains tasks which cannot be undertaken because you do not have access to the appropriate technology at that time. The following are a suggested set of headings, though you can devise your own, and major change costs pence, not pounds:

- phone calls
- at computer
- meetings (including agendas, paper, map)

- at school
- home
- contacts (notes of phone numbers, email, a plastic business card folder)
- information (a wallet file to keep articles, etc.)
- receipts (an envelope folder)
- ideas (for a project, holiday, the novel that you want to write).

Like the diary, including some contact details and an agreement to pay postage for its return is advisable.

Desk

It is a statement of the obvious that a desk is a workstation. Of course some leaders use it in other ways: as a barrier between them and staff or the public, and worst of all as a storage facility. The desk should be functional; there is no need to have paperclips aligned to magnetic north or your pens ranked in size order. Conversely, a cluttered desk with snaking cables going across it and cup rings on it is not a pleasant working environment. A simple checklist is to keep your desk clear, apart from when you are on task, of everything but equipment (e.g. computer and phone), supplies (e.g. staples, pens and paperclips) and some decoration (e.g. a family photo or an ornament).

Information

School leaders collect huge amounts of information: articles, circulars, minutes, policies and 'stuff'. The sad reality is that the dream of the paperless office never materialized. This requires a filing system; stacks or piles are not only inefficient but require large levels of cognitive RAM to operate.

Learning journal

Learning is a foundational process of both leadership and schools. Reflection and learning enhance the former and serve as a powerful model for the latter. Few if any of NCSL's leadership courses are deemed to be complete without a learning journal. Bruce Barnett (1995) argues that the capacity to reflect is enhanced when leaders keep a reflective journal and use a critical incident process to stimulate dialogue. He also notes that case study methods promote reflective skills. A key element of developing reflection is to link journal content with school experiences. The journal should be part of a trinity with the diary and the planner.

Tickler file

This a well-established organizational method which many people find hugely helpful. It requires a drawer of a filing cabinet with 43 suspension files in it. Twelve are labelled with the months of the year and the remaining numbered 1 to 31 for the days of the month.

For a given month sort items into the day folder for the day you want to deal with it. If something needs to be dealt with in a subsequent month place the item in the folder for that month. At the end of each month take the items from the next month's folder and distribute them as appropriate in the numbered day folder.

This provides a simple running reminder of when items, agendas, etc. can be found or need to be dealt with.

Review

Sadly no system works without the regular and disciplined input from its user. Without regular review and revision the tickler file becomes an irrelevant set of filing folders, the planner become a good idea and the diary survives out of necessity. Time management and its associated organization is not a peripheral leadership activity but is a core activity, which should be afforded a premium time slot. Ideally a minimum of an hour should be allocated. Many leaders find Friday afternoon a useful time to undertake this.

The time should split approximately as follows:

- *Review (30 minutes).* The planner is combed through and revised, for example the phone call list revised, contacts transferred to your database or file, receipts used as the basis of expense claims and information transferred to files or a 'to read' file.
- *Preview (15 minutes).* The diary for the next week is reviewed and amended. The tickler file is checked and items such as agendas transferred to the planner. Key action points are entered in to the appropriate section of the planner. Key tasks are prioritized; a useful rule is that a task can be done within ten minutes whereas a project is something that exceeds ten minutes. The latter will require a simple plan to execute it, which should include a budgeted time slot, involvement of colleagues where appropriate, and the gathering of resources. Again those two questions about being clear as to what it will look like when it is completed and what is the first action that needs to be taken are so useful.
- *Learning review (15 minutes).* Using your learning journal, reflect on two or three learning points and consider how these might impact your practice in the near future.

Better organization could allow more time to simply run on the spot. If improved organization is running in tandem with learning, the role of the leader is transformed. Stress is not just the product of a heavy workload but can also be exacerbated by what Roland Barth (2003) called 'routinisation'. Set in context he commented that:

> Learning is replenishing. We deplore teachers who do more of the same next September as they did this September and last September. I think it is equally unfortunate for the principal. After several years principals tend to switch onto 'automatic pilot' in PTA meetings, teacher evaluation sessions, and parent conferences – a sign of clinical death. Not only do teacher and student suffer, the principal suffers. Learning is an antidote to routinisation. (page 15)

8 Tool to tyrant

Imagine if every Thursday your shoes exploded if you tied them the usual way.
This happens to us all the time with computers, and nobody thinks of complaining.
(Jef Raskin)

The digital journey

Information and communication technology sneaked up on us whilst we were not looking.
It seemed relatively insignificant in its infancy. I remember the introduction of the first
computer into a Gloucester comprehensive school in the late 1970s. Afternoon tea was
served to staff and a mysterious black box, about the size of a kitchen cabinet, was unveiled
with the processing power of a speaking greetings card.

Within a decade I was using a BBC Master 128 complete with dot matrix printer for
word-processing, publishing rudimentary newsletters and certificates. Down the corridor
another BBC computer was working on the school timetable. My colleague set it to generate
solutions to staff allocation and room usage and then retired to the staffroom to eat his
lunch then teach two lessons of maths. And it had still not finished.

It was in the 1990s that the genie blew the cork out of the bottle and declined to return.
Several developments collided to transform the way we work radically and forever. Whilst
the IT revolution has many dimensions the following are particularly significant:

- The development of the personal computer, the Apple II in 1977 and the IBM PC in 1981.
  Increased sophistication at reduced cost has been seen as an entitlement ever since. Previously
  individuals had not had the time to explore and develop their relationship with a computer.
  Those who did have access to mainframes usually undertook specific tasks with prescriptive
  protocols after they had booked time; experimentation was not possible.
- The development and availability of graphical user interfaces. Friedman (2005) argues: 'the rise
  of the Windows-enabled PC, which really popularized personal computing, eliminated another

hugely important barrier: the limit on the amount of information that any single individual could amass, author, manipulate and diffuse' (page 55). Gone were the instantly forgettable codes replaced by a mouse-directed intuitive interface with icons. Information, whether as text, picture, video, music or voice, could be digitized, stored and edited.

- Connection through the shared protocols of the World Wide Web allied to the plumbing of the internet. The WWW was launched in 1991. Friedman (2005) noted that the number of users jumped from 600,000 to 40 million in five years and that at one stage the number of users was doubling every 53 days.

- The 'net generation': those young people who have grown up in a digital childhood and adolescence, handle this burgeoning technology with an ease and an approach which is different from that of the baby boomer generation. Wim Veen (2006) suggests that this generation skims computer screens instead of starting to read at the upper left corner of the window. Their goals are dictated by relevance and once identified they navigate quickly through digital environments. This net-generation multitasks processing multiple inputs of information at a time and creates their own meaning. Many will be aware of the frustration of watching TV with channel hopping offspring. The net-generation is able to deal with discontinuous visual information on the basis of implicit knowledge about information structures of visual information flows. Wim Veen has observed:

> From each program they pick up chunks and pieces of information and make logical connections based on the conceptual structure of the specific program, thus creating a meaningful whole out of discontinued information flows. This enables them to browse through multimedia content much faster than former generations. (This) net-generation has a non-linear approach towards learning. This approach also relates to the exploratory strategy they have been experiencing while playing games. They have been used to start playing the games without reading the manual first. They use resources only if there is a strict need to solve a problem rather than putting themselves in a 'learning mode' which starts with introductions and explanation on beforehand. This learning approach is at odds with most learning approaches at schools. At most schools learning is seen as a systematically planned and step-by-step designed approach from easy towards complex. The non-linear approach of today's kids helps them to learn in an active mode and as learning is widely accepted as an active mental process this skill helps learners to learn more efficiently and effectively. (pages 17–18)

This is their world, which they are progressively redesigning. The majority of those born before 1980 can only play catch-up and move through this 24/7 virtual world with a mechanical stiffness. In the area of ICT in schools the ignorant all too often try to lead the enlightened.

Connectivity is at the heartbeat of this digital revolution. Intriguingly the original conceptualization of data transfer was that 'The bandwidth on cable and phone lines was asymmetric: download rates far exceeded upload rates. The dogma of the age was that ordinary people had no need to upload; they were consumers, not producers' (Kelly, 2005, page 3).

Of course the computer is not the only digital portal. Connection comes through iPods, satellite navigation and of course the mobile phone. Toffler and Toffler (2006) point to the fact that technology develops with a self-sustaining impetus: 'Does anyone really think all these chips, computers, companies and Internet connections are going to vanish? Or that the world's 1,400,000,000 mobile phone users are going to throw their phones away? In fact, these, too, are daily morphing into more and more advanced and versatile digital devices' (page 6).

No place to run

Most senior leaders are 24/7, 365 connected. Their desktop at school is not discrete but linked through the school or local authority server. As a consequence remote access from home or even from a holiday destination is not only possible but also unremarkable. Many leaders use wifi enabled laptops and can use these in conference centres, at meetings and even in Starbucks. Significant amounts of the school's data can be carried in the pocket on a memory stick. The overwhelming majority of school leaders carry mobile phones. It is now a ritual at professional development events for the participants to switch on their phones at breaks and engage in animated conversations with the mother ship. We are in an era of total connection and for many there is no 'downtime'.

There is an interesting paradox between the high level of connectivity and the distance implicit in the technologies. Of course the iPod wearer is masked from the people centimetres away. The distance imposed by MSN, My Space or the phone carries an impact. In Chapter 2 the argument for developing empathy through mutual emulation was advanced. Goleman (2006) claims that the impact of over-reliance on these technologies which are not multi-sensory will result in social autism. He further comments that:

> A French report of a worldwide survey of 2.5 billion viewers in seventy-two countries revealed that in 2004 people spent an average of 3 hours 39 minutes each day watching television: Japan was the highest, with 4 hours and 25 minutes and the United States came a close second . . . The Internet and email have the same impact. A survey of 4,380 people in the United States found that for many the Internet has replaced television as the way that free time gets used. The math: for every hour spent using the Internet, their face to face contact with friends, co-workers and family fell by 24 minutes. We stay in touch at arm's length. (pages 8 and 9)

My space

Recent research into working with email has confirmed it as a source of increasing pressure in the workplace. Research carried out by the University of Glasgow (2007) discovered from a sample size of 177 that 34 per cent of workers felt stressed by the number of emails received; 50 per cent plus admitted to checking their inbox every hour and 35 per cent were checking their email every 15 minutes. The key stress points were first, the volume of traffic and second, that people felt obligated to reply quickly. Dr Renaud, a member of the team speaking to Beaumont (2007), concluded that:

> Email is an amazing tool, but it's got out of hand. You want to know what's in the message, especially if it's from family members, friends or your boss, so you break off from what you're doing to read the email. The problem is, when you go back to what you were doing you've lost your chain of thought. (page 23)

Anecdotal evidence from headteachers suggests that some are spending as much as two hours per day dealing with email.

There is a need to generate a structured way of handling email. The following are a number of key suggestions that will go some way towards taming the exponential inbox.

- Recognize that checking, handling and replying to email is a legitimate task. Many senior leaders have been happy to 'go through the post' in a formal session with their PA but somehow see dealing with email as an activity to be squeezed into gaps between other activities. It should be scheduled as a core daily task.
- It is recommended that you have a minimum of four email addresses. The first should be your main professional email along the lines of head@blackfield.foxshire.sch.uk. This is available to staff, parents and governors, and is printed on letterheads and school literature. All email sent to this address is routed via your PA and filtered in the same way as the post. The second one should be a restricted professional email address such as r.smith@blackfield.foxshire.sch.uk. It is given only to those whom you work with closely, for example members of the senior leadership team, key governors and LA colleagues. It is routed to your inbox and is for urgent and important email. Block email from anyone not on your list. The third one should be used when visiting websites which request an email address. Most leaders research a wide range of information and frequently these websites, which often request an email registration, become a source of spam. Simply route any email from this address into a separate box and periodically clear it out. In fact something like a hotmail account would do very adequately. The fourth email address should be your personal one for friends and family and it means just that. Simply do not be tempted to give this to business-related contacts.
- When you read email deal with those which can be responded to in a minute or less there and then. Move those which require a longer and more considered response to the appropriate folder (see below).
- Use folders. The story is told of someone who asked what system he should use because he had 29,000 emails in his inbox. The reply was almost any system would be an improvement! Folders are crucial; simply set them up for your main areas of activity and subdivide each into received and sent. Create two folders at the top of your list: action and hold. The action folder is subdivided into five folders for the days of the working week and that is when you deal with them. The hold folder is a parking space for information that you need to have on hand for the next week; any longer and it needs to be archived in the respective file. Some of this can also be

done automatically using rules and filters. The aim is to keep the inbox clear, or, as some have expressed it, defend the inbox.

- Set time aside to clear out these folders, monthly is about right. This is an area that needs working through otherwise you will end up with enormous email folders and you have simply moved the problem from the inbox.

- Do not store attachments in email folders; remove them and store them in appropriate folders in your documents. Trying to find an attachment stored with the email that came with it can be very time consuming.

- Switch off the automatic 'pop-ups' that alert you to the arrival of new email. Further, change the setting to automatically check for email to no more frequently than once per hour, preferably less often still.

- Use the spam setting ruthlessly to guard your inbox. Certainly marking the Department for Children, Schools and Families emails as spam will reduce the numbers you receive. However, this is not recommended as a strategy!

- Have a school protocol on the use of email. Problems arise around distribution lists. These should be agreed, for example amongst members of working parties, departments, etc. Arguably only one person, for example the headteacher's PA, should be able to use the whole staff distribution list. Anyone wanting to use this should apply to him or her for this to be distributed. Ban the use of the 'reply to all' function and require that any replies have to actually nominate the recipients.

- Use your 'out of office' function to provide some breathing space if you are likely to have a demanding day. It will notify people that they should not expect an immediate reply and should prevent people checking with you to see if you have received their email.

- Curb your enthusiasm to write at length. Brief emails are a blessing at both the beginning and the end of a process. Use a template for some replies.

- Be honest – if you know in your heart that you're never going to respond to an email, get it out of sight, archive it or just *delete it*. Guilt will not make you more responsive two months from now, otherwise you would respond now.

- A number of organizations have email-free Fridays. This is probably when they do the work. The main advantage is that this stops a sudden explosion of the inbox as colleagues try to clear their 'to do' list before going home for the weekend. Of course it does not stop outside email though of course you could expand the idea within a network of schools or the LA.

On the phone

In 1915 the US transcontinental telephone system had developed the capacity to handle three simultaneous voice calls. By the 1990s, individual Telstar satellites had enough capacity for nearly 100,000 telephone links. In 2007 a UN report, quoted in the *Herald Tribune* (2007), cited the total number of mobile phone subscribers as 2.68 billion. Very few senior leaders do not have a mobile phone and many have BlackBerry phones with email capability.

The central issue remains personal availability. The mobile for many people remains on 24/7 and of course there is no secretary to screen calls. There following are five key suggestions to tame this technology:

1. Assess your own relationship with your mobile. If you are away from the school is your role so pivotal that they must be able to contact you? Perhaps the better question is, 'What would happen if the school could not get in touch?' Figure 4.4 explored the issues of shared leadership and trust. Several years ago I was arranging an INSET day with a school and the head would only countenance one venue. This was a nearby hotel with a direct view of the school. For our sakes and for the growth of the organization there are times when it is useful to cut the technological umbilical cord.

2. Switch off the phone for most of the day. During the day most people will find a route to you if their need is sufficiently urgent, whilst many will just move on to other issues and realize that they did not really need to speak to you after all! Where callers are forced to use the school's landline call screening becomes possible. If you are routinely taking calls in the evening you are putting yourself at risk; it is time to get a life.

3. Having two phones works well. Have one phone for business and one for personal calls. It means that in the evenings, weekends and holidays you can enjoy social contact but screen out intrusive business contacts. You can always change the message on your business phone and explain that you will check it once a day though not when you are on your 'actual holiday'. Goleman (2006) records that in a survey of US workers on holiday 34 per cent checked in with their office so much that they came back stressed.

4. Limit the number of people to whom you give out your mobile number. Most people can reach you through your office number quite satisfactorily. Consider not putting your mobile on your business card.

5. The regulations about using a mobile in a car are strict and rightly so. Despite the legislation many drivers still continue to use their phone whilst driving without a hands-free system. Even if you do have such a system calls are still a distraction from the demanding task of driving. A hands-free call is best seen as exceptional rather than routine. Certainly an accident will significantly raise your levels of stress.

Disconnected

The burgeoning technologies have brought many benefits. Producing the manuscript for this book would have been so much less fun on a typewriter. The level of intrusion, however, must be tamed. The message of this chapter is about showing the technology who is in charge, to keep it firmly in its place as a tool and not allowing it to become a tyrant.

It is not appropriate for leaders to maintain excessive levels of open access. The core tasks of leadership are aligning people to the purpose of the organization and configuring the organization for the future. The leader should not be running a customer helpline.

9 Team games

Spectacular achievements are always preceded by unspectacular preparation.
(Roger Staubach)

Coming together is a beginning; keeping together is progress; working together is success. (Henry Ford)

The transition from the 1980s to the 1990s saw the evolution of senior management teams into senior leadership teams. In many cases this was little more than 'badge engineering'. Many school-based teams have problems rooted in their creation, operation and maintenance. Dysfunctional teams can soon lose credibility within the school community and also reduce leadership capacity. Frequently they can absorb time and energy and the headteacher can feel as if a second front has opened up. Conversely, a well-founded team sponsors innovation, maintains a corporate vision, is mutually supportive, engages with change and its leadership, provides a wellspring for succession and is the incarnation of the school's value system.

Much of the literature on teams is drawn from research and writing on commercial and industrial project teams, for example Belbin (1981), Tuckman (1965) or even Irving Janis (1972). Most school teams are not constituted in the same way but tend to be semi-permanent and with a 'catch-all' brief. Frequently they are not specifically created but are the construct of the passage of time. Most inbound headteachers inherit 'teams' that have a membership based on seniority, role or salary scale. The composition of these teams often reflects a desire to capture key school activities in the form of representative personnel. However, like the throw of the dice this can as easily produce a 'one' as a 'six'.

Arguably there are a number of factors which should be addressed if a team is to enhance capacity and school effectiveness:

- *Purpose* – it should have a clear purpose that is clearly understood by both the members of the team and the wider school community.

- *Roles* – the contributions and roles of its members should be explicit rather than implicit.
- *Politics and personalities* – the politics of the members should be understood and challenge offered when appropriate.
- *Development and maintenance* – there should be an ongoing process of development and maintenance taking place, which is central rather than an afterthought.
- *Learning teams* – all teams should be 'learning teams' which source the organizational understanding of teamworking. In the case of a senior leadership team it should be an exemplar to other teams within the school.

Purpose

> Change has accelerated – the fact that this is a cliché makes it no less true. In today's hyper-competitive business environment, expertise lasts nanoseconds before something new appears. As a result, only well-integrated teams can effectively handle the sheer mass of information and solve the complex problems that come their way. (Burnham, 2003, page 40)

Many members of teams believe that the purpose of their team is self-evident. Surprisingly that is far from the case. Unlike many project-based teams, educational teams are part time. The members of the team 'donate' time around doing their 'proper job', which might be finance, discipline, curriculum, buildings, HR, timetabling and perhaps even a bit of teaching. This has a considerable impact on how the team operates when it comes together in a formal capacity. In the work with the London Challenge two activities of teams seemed to predominate: first, therapy, where the problems and pressures of members were unloaded. This was usually accompanied by tea and biscuits. As an aside one team actually had a huge teapot in the middle of the table and used a copy of the 1988 Educational Reform Act as a mat! The second activity was reporting back, where team members brought others up to speed accompanied by questions for clarification – indeed one team responded that they had not made a decision as a team for three years.

The distinction between a work group and a team relates to performance. A work group relies on the individual inputs of its members. An effective team is constituted to achieve more than the simple sum of the contributions of its constituent members.

Katzenbach and Smith (2004) have identified three basic types of teams:

1. *teams that recommend things* – task forces or project groups;
2. *teams that run things* – groups that oversee some significant functional activity;
3. *teams that make or do things* – manufacturing operations or marketing groups.

They go on to assert that: 'Considering the extra level that teams can achieve, the authors believe that teams will become the primary work unit in high-performance organizations' (page 2).

Most senior leadership teams operate with Katzenbach and Smith's first and second categories. When operating in the first category the power of the teams is that they can solve problems and, in Fullan's words, ensure 'more good things happen and fewer bad things happen' (2001, page 4). Perhaps more importantly the team can design new possibilities, for example new approaches to learning, innovative approaches to the curriculum, community centred education and remodelling of the workforce.

When educational teams are operating as a fulcrum of change or innovation they face the problem of implementation. Most senior leadership teams meet formally once a week for perhaps two hours. If the team generates ideas other staff are frequently required to execute these. Katzenbach and Smith (2004) argue that the significant issue is about missing the hand-off. As the idea is passed it can also become fainter like the photocopy of the photocopy of the photocopy. Unless those implementing the change are involved at an early stage imposition can generate resentment and hostility. Meanwhile in many instances the originating team has moved on to other ideas.

The second category, teams that run things, can also be problematical. There is a great deal of 'plate spinning' taking place alongside a wide range of other demanding tasks. This managerial role requires a consistency of approach rather than random sampling. The theme of consistency is a constant refrain amongst leadership teams. All too frequently campaigns are intermittently waged against litter, homework, punctuality, school uniform, discipline, smoking, bullying and even classroom observation. These 'plates' are then left spinning until they start to wobble again and a new campaign is started. Perhaps the energy and creativity of the team should generate a solution, which includes the maintenance of an approach or system. Katzenbach and Smith (2004) suggest that often such functions are better served by the creation of working groups which operate with tight agendas and protocols.

The central question here is 'What is the purpose of this particular team?' Perhaps this could be reframed as 'If the team did not meet what would change?'

Contribution

Most leaders are familiar with the (now almost venerable) work of Meredith Belbin (1981). The original list of eight roles has had that of 'specialist' added, which unlike the others is not linked to personality type. Belbin's conclusion is that teams work best when there is a balance of primary roles and when team members know their roles, work to their strengths and actively manage weaknesses.

Overall	Belbin role
Leading	Coordinator Shaper
Doing	Implementer Completer/finisher
Thinking	Monitor/evaluator Plant Specialist
Socializing	Resource/investigator Team worker

Table 9.1 Belbin roles

To achieve the best balance, there should be:

- one coordinator or shaper (not both) for leader;
- a plant to stimulate ideas;
- a monitor/evaluator to maintain honesty and clarity;
- one (or more) implementer, team worker, resource investigator or completer/finisher to make things happen.

Belbin's work has been a mainstay of management and leadership programmes since the 1980s. Despite their familiarity with so many leaders, many teams still fail because they are overstocked with particular 'roles'. For example, many secondary deputies were appointed for their managerial skills especially as timetablers. In time they have moved into headship and gathered deputies around them with similar skills and perspectives. These teams are hugely gifted in the 'doing' category but are often conservative in terms of original thinking and a little short on the interpersonal skills front.

Teams should be aware of their composition utilizing Belbin's analysis or some similar personality inventory. Where there is an imbalance this needs to be confronted and compensation made either through appointment or by a team member stepping up from a secondary strength. Certainly each member should be clear about what it is that he or she both brings and needs from the team.

Politics and personalities

This is often where the 'team theory' can degenerate into the script of a 'soap opera'. Some teams can be isolated from their wider communities and perceived as aloof whilst others can be inappropriately permeable. The following case study illustrates the minefield that can be created by webs of relationships (this one is absolutely true but again anonymized).

Case study: Toxic team

Jack needed a supportive senior leadership team to take the school forward. The reality, whilst not 'premier league', looked workable. There was an initial discussion about strengths and weaknesses using a SWOT analysis and a common set of values was agreed along the lines of 'raising achievement'.

Some of the problems became apparent early on whilst some members adopted a more clandestine Machiavellian approach. The outcome was a cauldron of dysfunction and the loss of credibility with staff. Jack would have liked a delete button but two years down the road there were too many ongoing issues to make major changes. Eventually criticism was made of the leadership and management of the school which resulted in a change of the head and some of the key players. The following is the cast list of that senior leadership team.

- *David: deputy head* – a 'wheeler-dealer' with a personal network. His main role was the management and organization of the curriculum, which was operated from an extremely pragmatic stance. In some cases the number of staff available dictated the numbers of periods for a particular subject. It was questionable whether Year 9 needed three periods on careers every week. His motto was explicitly stated as 'knowledge is power', which is not the basis for team play. Many staff believed him to be vindictive.
- *Julia: deputy head* – a maternal figure, everybody's agony aunt. In reality an accomplished plotter and schemer with a social network penetrating into local educational power structures. Dissatisfied with the previous head she had invited a senior LA adviser for a meal and undertaken a powerful demolition job. This was the precursor for Jack's predecessor taking early retirement. Jack found that old habits die hard.
- *Alan: assistant head* – there was a mismatch between his friendly façade and the staff's almost universal dislike of him. Towards the end of his first week as head, Jack had dealt with an inherited complaint from a parent. Alan had disciplined a Year 10 girl and had physically blocked her in his office. It transpired that Alan was the school's Lothario and had made advances to several female staff and precipitated the departure of one by leaving notes on her windscreen. He was also a somewhat turgid thinker.
- *Peter: assistant head* – a key player heading up data management, timetable and the school's application for specialist status. Greatly valued for his intellectual capabilities and creative thinking. Sadly these were not matched by his integrity and interpersonal skills. Previously a head of department his promotion had provided the opportunity to intimidate other staff, especially female staff. There had been a number of formal complaints made against him. Jack was told in confidence that Peter was opening his email in advance.
- *Anne: Head of English* – a thoroughgoing professional but very people centred. She had been confused by the duplicity of some of the team and hurt by some of the 'put downs'. The consequence of being in a toxic team is that she no longer made much contribution.

- *Robert: community coordinator* – very supportive but little respected by teaching staff. There was a perception that he was lazy and did not carry the same workload as they did.
- The problem for Jack was that he did not have the personal capacity of staffing or resources to change this dysfunctional team. Whilst it would have been painful to make required changes at an early stage, with the benefit hindsight this would have been the prudent course of action.

The above case study has been included to emphasize that in developing and working with teams there can be other forces at work. The intensely personal nature of some of the issues outlined is difficult to deal with. Challenging these will often be met with denial. Frequently headteachers will prevaricate in dealing with them and they become the so-called 'elephant in the room'. A failure to engage with these issues will have a disastrous impact on the effectiveness of the team and generate high levels of stress.

In the previous section the necessity for building teams with people of different personality styles was explored. Returning to Chapter 1, personality types in terms of 'obsessive', 'narcissistic' and 'erotic' were examined. The point was strongly made that we all have these dimensions; problems start with team members when one of these dimensions is exhibited in excess. The 'obsessive' team members will tend to be irritated by free-ranging discussion and want excessive amounts of fine detail tied down before moving forward. The extreme 'erotic' team members will want feathers unruffled, can become uncomfortable with heated debate and may also have difficulty in making decisions if these have a negative impact on people. In all probability it is the 'narcissistic' team members who will create serious turbulence. They are not team players and cooperation is anathema to them. Their lack of empathy can leave other team members bruised and resentful. Appointing a senior leader in a school who is narcissistic in style may be appropriate in a particular context but this is extremely unlikely to build a team.

Jim Collins, in his book *Good to Great* (2001), highlights the importance of getting the team right with following metaphor:

The executives who ignited the transformations from good to great did not first figure out where to drive the bus and then get people to take it there. No, they first got the right people on the bus (and the wrong people off the bus) and then figured out where to drive it. They said, in essence, 'Look, I don't really know where we should take this bus. But I know this much: If we get the right people on the bus, the right people in the right seats, and the wrong people off the bus, then we'll figure out how to take it someplace great.' (page 41)

He later added:

> For no matter what we achieve, if we don't spend the vast majority of our time with people we love and respect, we cannot possibly have a great life. But if we spend the vast majority of our time with people we love and respect – people we really enjoy being on the bus with and who will never disappoint us – then we will almost certainly have a great life, no matter where the bus goes. The people we interviewed from the good-to-great companies clearly loved what they did, largely because they loved who they did it with. (page 62)

Many leaders are desperately moving the direction indicator on the front of the bus in the hope that members of their team with 'leadership ASBOs' or who are sat in comfort by the heater outlet will change or leave. Whilst it cannot be said unequivocally that this will not happen the odds are on the side of the status quo.

In the changing rooms

Most team games are followed by analysis, some informal whilst showering, some formal and exacting. It would be unthinkable in any team sport to just play. Amongst leadership teams in school such analysis is still relatively rare. There is a need to have a commitment to excellence and then to ask how we can get even better. Rarer still is the ability to capture that learning and share it with other teams whether it is 'triumph or disaster'. This process of knowledge capture and knowledge management is discussed further in Chapter 11.

The analysis of play is derived from a clear understanding of team purpose and clarity of each individual's role; arbitration is against the agreed rules, success is applauded and losing is not tolerated. Plans are laid for the team to be devastatingly good on its next outing. A team which is not achieving coherence and which is satisfied with coming second in each game it plays is well on the way to relegation.

Educational leadership teams need to learn something of that same passion for winning. Roles must be clear, rules established and those who are not playing the game should be called to account. Time must be given for team development; being an effective team player is not an allocation but a hard won skill.

A simple analysis of performance using WWW (What Went Well) and EBI (Even Better If) can pay huge dividends. There are also more sophisticated tools to help with understanding your team. One proving of huge value is Motivational Mapping (www.motivationalmaps.com) or the team programmes run by the National College for School Leadership: Working Together for Success and Developing Capacity for Sustained Improvement.

Two years ago in the context of Working Together for Success I recorded a DVD to demonstrate the GROW coaching model. The client spoke of ongoing problems with a deputy. This had come to a head over the introduction of staff rotas. He had been challenged over the rather cavalier attitude of the deputy and in the face of comment from staff and governors he was put on the spot to resolve the situation. When the DVD has been shown there is an audible gasp when the reply to the question 'How long has the problem been going on?' comes back as 'Three years'. It would be easy to judge this head but that type of response is by no means exceptional. More pertinent is to reflect on the inevitable poverty of the team, which has been undermined by that relationship and also the stress on that headteacher and probably the deputy as well.

10 The only alternative

The significant problems we have cannot be solved at the same level of thinking with which we created them. (Albert Einstein (attributed))

When life seems chaotic, you don't need people giving you easy answers or cheap promises. There might not be any answers to your problems. What you need is a safe place where you can bounce with people who have taken some bad hops of their own. (Real Live Preacher.com weblog (accessed 12/8/2003))

Houston, we have a problem

John Swigert and James Lovell, who with Fred Haise made up the crew of the US Apollo 13 moon flight, used (almost) these phrases to report a major technical problem back to Houston ground control:

> Swigert: OK, Houston, we've had a problem here.
>
> Duke: This is Houston. Say again, please.
>
> Lovell: Houston, we've had a problem . . . We've had a main B bus undervolt.

This quotation is now used in an almost humorous sense to report problems; this was obviously not the situation when Swigert and Lovell used it on 14 April 1970 (intriguingly Swigert replaced Thomas Mattingly as command module pilot just hours before the mission began after it was found that Mattingly had no immunity after exposure to German measles). The very word 'problem' has huge power even if it is framed as a negative, for example 'that's not a problem'. Whilst it can be used to describe events ranging from mild irritation to cataclysm it can trigger both physiological change and different ways of thinking. Using the word 'problem' or its synonyms such as 'difficulty', 'trouble', 'crisis', 'dilemma' and 'predicament' usually set alarm bells ringing and move us to a heightened state of physical and mental alert.

Consider the following case studies.

Case study: Hot water

It is the beginning of January, in fact the second day back at school. Andrew, the headteacher of a medium sized rural comprehensive school, is at his desk replying to emails. The site manager enters the office to inform him that the school heating system has packed in and that it will be three days before it can be fixed.

It is extremely cold and the obvious course of action is to send the students home and close the school until after the weekend. Immediately the management team swings into gear and the process of temporary closure is started.

Buses are ordered, newsletters are printed, parents contacted, the LEA informed, the password for announcements via the local radio station located. The boiler engineers, fortunately under contract to the LEA, are engaged. By 2.00 pm the entire process has been completed.

Case study: Ambush

Helen accepted her second headship in a school which was struggling at many levels. The school had served its community well, although a marketing campaign focusing on a motif as a 'caring school' had resulted in an imbalance of pupils with special educational needs. The numbers and the intake had been sliced by competition from two single-sex secondary schools still basking in the afterglow of earlier days as grammar schools. The loss of the sixth form, eight years previously, had conferred relegation status on the school in the eyes of teaching staff and potential client groups alike.

The previous headteacher had been overtaken by the pace of change and been granted an honourable discharge. There had been three attempts to appoint a new head, which had produced a great deal of uncertainty amongst staff and parents. The context and circumstances of the school had led to a celebration of failure. More dangerous was the perception by many staff and even some officers of the LEA of the school as a victim. A presentation on 'value added' had prompted one teacher to counter concerns over performance with the comment 'What do you expect with these children?' At a stroke, this subverted the entire message of 'value added' and confirmed the member of staff in an image of professional emasculation.

A month after being appointed Helen was invited to a Friday afternoon meeting with a link adviser and a senior LEA adviser. The meeting, initially cordial, degenerated into one which was coercive. Data relating to the school was produced which indicated a far more serious situation than had been presented at her interview. The expectation was made clear that she would sort the situation out in double-quick time particularly as an Ofsted Inspection could well be imminent.

$\Rightarrow$

> Helen left the meeting feeling both isolated and a heavy weight of pressure. She was going to have to drive change and precipitate a revolution rather than engender an evolution of change. Her field of vision had narrowed to statistically summarized student outcomes. Helen's mind was reeling as twenty years' professional experience became funnelled through a small aperture of expectation.

These two case studies are anonymized, drawn from real-life situations, and are very different in terms of resolution. The first, with its crisis over the heating system, was time limited, the crisis externally imposed, the response procedures were largely prescribed, the reasons for taking action were self-evident and there was a clear end in view. It belongs in the category of 'urgent and important'. Emergency planning brought focus on the crisis and offered the luxury of excluding almost every other activity.

The second case study was more challenging. Helen was confronted with a significant realignment of her professional relationships; partnership had been eclipsed by accountability. She was now expected not only to come up with ideas but also to generate concrete outcomes in terms of student achievement by the LEA officers. Her time-frame had changed from tomorrow to today with the option of building a team appearing a luxury. The school was not a very coherent organization. Poor leadership had been the hallmark of her predecessor and staff had learned how to justify poor teaching by understanding themselves as postcode victims. At a national or local level there is little consensus about the causes of underachievement or indeed its resolution. Since the 1988 Education Reform Act there has been an overwhelming focus on school improvement. In the main, schools are more rigorously managed and there have been improvements. There is, however, no template which can be overlaid on a school and will inevitably lead to sustained high achievement. The case study leaves Helen driving away from her meeting with the LEA advisers and facing a weekend of reflection, her thoughts tumbling around her mind in disconnected manner.

Underpinning the second case study is stress. There is a strong element of personal challenge and professional risk. The argument has been made that such stress changes the way we think. In this context it is important to highlight three key areas:

1. *Focus* – when we are overwhelmed by issues, problems or circumstances we frequently lose clarity. Our brains are set to encourage self-preservation through flight or fight; reasoned problem solving rapidly becomes a secondary activity. We need to define the problem we are trying to solve. For example, school leaders frequently talk about a desire that every student achieves their full potential. On the basis that we allegedly use about 5 per cent of our brains, goodness knows what that is. A phrase such as 'Achieving high standards for all' actually has little meaning and would serve as a very poor point of focus.

2. *Solution* – stress and pressure are likely to narrow the possible courses of action. Consider for a moment that frequently heard phrase 'the only alternative'. This must be one of the best examples of an oxymoron in the English language. If there is an 'alternative' then the word 'only' cannot be readily attached to the phrase. There is a need to broaden thinking and generate a range of potential solutions.
3. *Action* – there must be a clear strategy for implementation. The two extremes of making a knee-jerk response or, at the other end of the spectrum, entering into a state of leadership fibrillation must be avoided. Sometimes just asking two basic questions can make a significant difference: first, 'What will the task/situation look like when it's completed?' and second, 'What is the first step I need to take to make things happen?'

An alternative approach was suggested by David Brent, in the TV series *The Office*, who argued that when you are confronted by a difficult problem, you can solve it more easily by reducing it to the question 'What would the Lone Ranger do in this situation?' Moving swiftly on!

Problem Solving Team Building

A tool which has been widely used in work with senior leadership teams through the London Challenge initiative and then later through the Training and Development Agency's remodelling initiative is PSTB (Problem Solving Team Building). It is also known as the Seven-Step Process. This simple methodology addresses the key areas of focus, solution and action. It can be used with established teams or by a one-off team gathered for a specific purpose. It works well for concrete problems rather than those with philosophical roots. Normally it is intended to run for predetermined periods ranging from 20 to 45 minutes; for most purposes 30 minutes seems to work well. I did come across one team who employed the process for over two hours. I remain unclear whether they were superhuman or merely misguided!

The process depends on a team adopting particular roles:

- *The problem owner* – defines the problem, provides relevant background information, and makes decisions in order to select from the team's proposals.
- *The facilitator* – the guardian of the process, with which he or she must be fully conversant, who keeps everyone on time, process, and records the output (unless a volunteer offers to scribe!).
- *The team resources* – the established team or specifically gathered team. These people generate ideas and provide constructive critical thinking.

This problem solving technique has been widely used in industrial and commercial contexts. The outline in Figure 10.1 is taken from the Training and Development Agency's remodelling resources and is for a 30-minute session (reproduced by kind permission of the TDA).

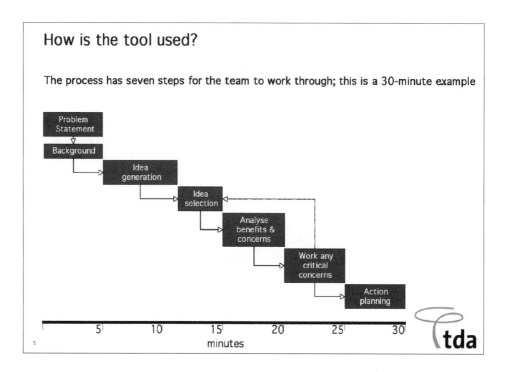

How is the tool used?

The process has seven steps for the team to work through; this is a 30-minute example

Figure 10.1 30-minute PSTB

If the group is not familiar with the process then the facilitator describes it briefly and then provides support as the group moves through the steps. A flipchart is an advantage.

- *Steps 1 and 2: Problem statement and background (five minutes).* The problem owner describes the issue and the resources ask questions for clarification. At the end of Step 2 the aim is to write up on a flipchart the problem statement framed as a simple 'How do I . . .' question. It is important that this is 'tight', as a diffuse question is likely to lead to confusion later in the process.
- *Steps 3 and 4: Idea generation and idea selection (10 minutes).* Step 3 is a classic brainstorm activity. The resources are asked to produce as many potential solutions in five minutes as they can; the problem owner can, of course, contribute. In true brainstorming tradition, no idea is a bad idea and there should be no discussion of the merits of the various contributions at this stage. The easiest way to capture these is for the facilitator to scribe these on a flipchart, or post-its can be used. Usually some grouping of ideas helps as there is often duplication or similarity amongst some of the suggestions. In Step 4 the problem owner selects two or three ideas that appeal. The problem owner should keep the remaining ones for further use.
- *Step 5: Benefits and concerns (five minutes).* For each selected idea the benefits and concerns are considered by all except, of course, the facilitator, who remains in charge of the process not the content. Dividing a flipchart into two columns is an easy way to tackle this. Of course if

there are no benefits, however obvious it may seem, it is questionable that the idea should be used!

- *Step 6: Critical concerns (five minutes)*. The group explores the concerns from Step 5. If there are 'killer concerns', that is concerns that cannot be overcome, then another idea should be selected. General concerns should be reviewed quickly and awareness raised over potential pitfalls and ways to overcome them identified.
- *Step 7: Action plan (five minutes)*. The intention is to produce a simple action plan which identifies a few of the steps to be taken, the person/persons who will take the action and the timescale for the action.

This is a deceptively simple process but the structure ties the problem solving activity into key principles and secures a better outcome. At the end of 30 minutes the problem owner should emerge with two or three ideas, an awareness of potential difficulties and a rudimentary action plan.

Two years ago whilst I was facilitating a New Visions (early headship) programme one head arrived distressed after receiving disappointing KS3 SATS data for mathematics for his school. Initially he perceived the situation as hopeless and viewed resignation as a likely option. A 30-minute PSTB was used with the rest of the group serving as resources. The situation was transformed and the head left with a bundle of flipchart sheets, and confidence and resolve to tackle what only a few hours previously had been an impossible situation.

Beyond problem solving

Problem solving is very much in the 'urgent and important' area of leadership and management. Creative thinking (I could not bring myself to use the term 'blue sky' thinking') is in the 'not urgent but important' category of the task of leading schools and other organizations. The ability to create innovative ways of working and organizing learning is germane to surviving and thriving in our rapidly changing world. It is important to note that creativity is about innovation rather than invention. For example, soon after the advent of cyanoacrylate adhesives (superglue), it was noted that if you weren't careful, you could glue your fingers together with it. This problem – a permanent skin bond – was soon seen as a solution, too. Surgeons in Vietnam began to use superglue to glue wounds together. Very often we have the parts but need to assemble them differently. Powered flight was developed by two bicycle mechanics!

There are a number of techniques and processes which can be deployed to support individuals and teams to think creatively; some readers may have used *Six Thinking Hats* by Edward De Bono (1999). In essence individuals/teams wear imaginary coloured hats and deliberately choose to adopt a particular frame of thinking which can break down entrenched positions. The following is a synopsis of the thinking styles and their associated coloured hats:

- *White hat* – the focus is on data. The information that you have is examined and analysed. Look for gaps in your knowledge, and try either to fill them or to take account of them. Past trends are examined and extrapolations are made from the data.
- *Red hat* – this thinking style is about feelings and intuition, gut reactions and emotion. Empathy is deployed to consider how others might react especially those who do not fully understand your reasoning.
- *Black hat* – using black hat thinking the negative dimension is considered. The issue is examined cautiously and defensively. Attempts are made to understand why the solution might not work. This is important because it can highlight the weak points in a plan. It allows you to eliminate them, alter them or prepare contingency plans to counter them. Black hat thinking helps to make your plans 'tougher' and more resilient. It can also help you to spot fatal flaws and risks before you embark on a course of action. Black hat thinking is one of the real benefits of this technique, as many successful people get so used to thinking positively that often they cannot see problems in advance. This leaves them under-prepared to deal with difficulties in their scheme or project.
- *Yellow hat* – the yellow hat stance helps you to think positively. It is the optimistic viewpoint that concentrates on the benefits and value of the decision. Yellow hat thinking helps you to keep going against the odds.
- *Green hat* – the green hat is symbolic for creativity. This is where creative solutions to a problem can be developed. It is a freewheeling way of thinking, in which ideas are not critiqued.
- *Blue hat* – blue hat thinking is very much about control of the process. This is the hat worn by people chairing meetings. When running into difficulties because ideas are running dry, they may direct activity into green hat thinking. When contingency plans are needed, they will ask for black hat thinking, etc.

Sometimes simply changing our focus can liberate our thinking and allow the consideration of new possibilities for a situation either as an individual or as a team.

A further process which is well established and extremely powerful is 'Appreciative Enquiry' (or AI, an abbreviation rooted in the transatlantic spelling of 'enquiry'). The concept was developed by David Cooperrider and Suresh Srivista from the Weatherhead School of Management at Case Western University, Ohio in 1987. Recently it has been detailed in the *Appreciative Inquiry Handbook* (Cooperrider et al., 2003). Fry writing in the foreword to the book summarizes the process:

> The practice of Appreciative Inquiry is much more about a way of being – a holistic posture of standing in front of a situation (of engaging with others) with the will and curiosity to look into what there is to be valued in order to imagine most boldly what is possible for the future. The will to look for the best of what is will be reciprocated in mutual recognition and positive human connections. The curiosity will reveal new ideas and exciting experiments. (page xi)

It is argued that the problem solving approach tends to look backwards rather than forwards and it frequently generates defensiveness rather than energy and enthusiasm for change.

Appreciative Enquiry is frequently described as a four-stage process. Cooperrider (2003) offers a pragmatic description; I have added a commentary to each of the stages, which serves to underscore how the brain is being deployed.

In Stage 1 (discovery), an issue might be identified and then through interview or data gathering previous best practice is captured. It is about seeking inspirational narrative. It is argued that even organizations which are in extremis have experience of success, good practice or exemplary leadership. From this interviewing and data gathering phase important topics or themes emerge.

The power of this stage is that it sets the stage for creativity. Exploring new possibilities is less likely to develop from a platform of failure and despondency. The sharing of success sets the brain up for engaging in creativity. Thomas White, president of GTE Telephone Operations, raised the following question: 'In the long run what is likely to be more useful: demoralizing a successful workforce by concentrating on their failures or helping them over their last few hurdles by building a bridge with their successes?' (Cooperrider et al., 2003).

In Stage 2 (dream), participants gather in groups of six (it could well be a senior leadership team) to share common themes and important topics. They then work together on dreaming, envisioning an image of an ideal future which is powerful because it is grounded in reality and based on actual examples of excellence. It may well be helpful to draw this ideal future, a practice which has been powerfully used in a number of schools. Surprisingly, drawing captures dimensions which words alone can miss.

At this stage the creative right side of the brain is engaged and has been set up for creative thinking.

In Stage 3 (design), dreams or provocative propositions are converted into tangible projects, actions or experiments. There are seven underpinning principles of the design phase:

1. inclusive
2. aspirational
3. continuity (building on past success)
4. innovative
5. re-enquiry (make predictions about what will work)
6. home-grown
7. chaordic (working on the boundary of chaos and order).

These projects or actions are typically shared with the whole organization.

The design stage is a carefully crafted planning process. It deploys left-brain thinking to ensure that actions are carefully analysed and thought through. Of course this is not to the exclusion of maintaining good relationships with personnel directly and indirectly involved.

In Stage 4 (delivery), the term originally used was destiny. It may well be that delivery better describes the process. It is very much about project management. Formative review is appropriate because change and innovation are at the heart of the process. New things are being undertaken with new teams and structures and with colleagues deploying new skills. Empowerment without enablement is at the best misjudged and at the worst cynical.

Postscript

All solution-focused activity engages with change processes. John West-Burnham and Max Coates (2005) argue that: 'One of the great oxymorons is that it is possible to manage change. By definition change is so complex and involves so many fundamental questions that it has to involve leadership. It also needs management – but only in the sense of consolidating and sustaining change' (page 107). Their comments serve as a timely reminder that implementing change is an extreme leadership activity. The intricacies of leading change are beyond the remit of this book. The intention here is to inform and challenge leaders about the impact of their personal mental frame and the consequences of the processes employed by either design or default. Cooperrider (2003) provides an intriguing epitaph which he entitles the Pygmalion Effect:

> In the classic Pygmalion study, teachers are lead to believe on the basis of 'credible' information that some of their students possess exceptionally high potential while others do not. So the teachers are led, on the basis of some expert opinion, to hold a positive image (PI) of some students and a negative image (NI), or expectance of others. Unknown to the teachers, however, is the fact that the so-called high-potential students were selected at random. In objective terms, all student groups were equivalent in potential and were merely dubbed high, regular or low potential. As the experiment unfolds, differences quickly emerge – not on the basis of any innate intelligence factor or some other predisposition, but solely on the basis of the manipulated expectancy of the teacher. Over time subtle changes among students evolve into clear differences, as the high-PI students begin to significantly overshadow all others in actual achievement.

> The key lesson is that cognitive capacities are cued and shaped by images projected through another's expectations. For example, what is seen is believed. As a result actions take on a whole new tone based on the perceived image. The resulting differential behavioural treatment, in turn, makes the people receiving this treatment begin to respond to the positive images that others have of them. (pages 10–11)

A concluding comment, again from Cooperrider, 2003, under the delightfully named heliotropic hypothesis: 'Human systems have an observable tendency to evolve in the direction of those positive images that are the brightest and boldest, most illuminating and promising' (page 12).

11 It's not what you know but who you know

Our experience is that to be useful knowledge needs to be refreshed frequently. Perhaps this is why companies that sell mineral water market their products as 'natural spring water' and 'bottled at source'. When was the last time you bought mineral water that was 'drawn from the lake'? (Collison and Parcell, 2004, page 19)

Knowledge is of two kinds. We know a subject ourselves, or we know where we can find information on it. (Samuel Johnson)

Connection not collection

Howard Kennedy (2007), the Training and Development Agency Director of Change, quoted a series of challenging statistics at a recent launch event for the Innovation Unit. He commented that a week's content of the *New York Times* would contain more information than a person would come across in a lifetime in the eighteenth century. It was also stated that technical knowledge is currently doubling every two years but that by 2010 it will double every 72 hours.

Statistics like these coupled with our daily experience suggest that our existing approaches to handling knowledge are teetering on the brink of collapse. Renaissance man was able to range freely across the sciences and the arts and achieve a comprehensive grasp of current understanding. The knowledge explosion has driven specialization with its ever-present danger of the specialist becoming isolated by the complexity of his or her understanding. Knowledge is increasingly less about collection and more about connection. An individual will not have the capacity to be the repository of all relevant knowledge but a well-networked team will be at a significant advantage. Teams hold a range of expertise and in turn link to wider networks where knowledge is held. Organizations are increasingly talking in terms of knowledge capture and knowledge management and developing new ways of collaboration.

Schools generally, though the picture is beginning to change, have lagged behind in the field of knowledge management. Senior leaders are still appointed as 'renaissance figures', valued for their all-round competence and of course their ability to teach. Ironically, schools are perceived as fulcra of learning within our society and yet seldom have a vision for organizational learning. Frequently they bring in experts to develop staff and yet often there is little confidence in the outcomes and as a consequence the impact is ephemeral. Schools have a highly qualified workforce and yet are all too seldom nurtured by their own resources. Learning networks are developing like a rash but often they are more about sharing resources than about creating knowledge.

Lead Learners

On an early headship programme one participant produced a photo of his school sign where he was identified as the 'Lead Learner'. This produced levels of bewilderment amongst some of the other participants and muted derision amongst others. In many ways his sentiments were laudable; in others they did not go far enough. The very title re-established the hierarchical view of educational leadership that he was trying so hard to dismantle.

Peter Senge (1990) talks about the leader as teacher and develops his argument from Max de Pree's (1990) injunction that the first responsibility of a leader is to define reality. Many leaders draw inspiration and spiritual reserves from their sense of stewardship: 'much of the leverage leaders can actually exert lies in helping people achieve more accurate, more insightful and more *empowering* views of reality' (Senge, 1990, page 353). Building on an existing 'hierarchy of explanation' leaders, Senge argues, can influence people's view of reality at four levels: events, patterns of behaviour, systemic structures and the 'purpose story'. By and large most managers and leaders tend to focus on the first two of these levels and this sets the tone of the organization. The key conversations are about what happened or what is going to happen or who did what or who needs to do some task or activity. Leaders in learning organizations attend to all four, 'but focus predominantly on purpose and systemic structure. Moreover they "teach" people throughout the organization to do likewise' (Senge, 1990, page 353). This allows them to see 'the big picture' and to appreciate the structural forces that condition behaviour. By attending to purpose, leaders can cultivate an understanding of what the organization (and its members) is seeking to become. One of the issues here is that leaders often have strengths in one or two of the areas but are unable, for example, to develop systemic understanding. Leaders need to be able to capture and summarize what is happening and then to communicate it clearly in a way that is open to challenge and further improvement.

'Leader as teacher' is not about 'teaching' people how to achieve their vision. It is about fostering learning, for everyone. Such leaders help people throughout the organization develop systemic understandings. Accepting this responsibility is the antidote to one of the most common downfalls of otherwise gifted teachers – losing their commitment to the truth. (Senge, 1990, page 356)

Pre-eminently the leader is the conductor, encouraging collaboration, harmony, creativity and also virtuoso performances. He or she knows how to conduct and knows the range and contribution of every instrument and musician but is unlikely to play every instrument. Leaders have to create and manage creative tension – especially around the gap between vision and reality. Mastery of such tension allows for a fundamental shift. It enables the leader to see the truth in changing situations.

There is liberation in the realization that knowledge does not have to be held by the individual leader and that not knowing something is of considerably less significance than knowing somebody who does. There is a tension in that senior leaders are still expected to be aware of the content of their profession and there is less emphasis on their mastery of process. Knowledge management is an inescapable necessity and a core skill but is still at the stage of genesis.

Developing knowledge permeable organizations

Schools like other organizations are facing significant challenges and are implicitly and explicitly being redesigned. As organizations they have a pressing need for knowledge and its management. The term is being routinely used to capture outcomes of learning beyond data or information. It is understood as dynamic and eclectic. Collison and Parcell (2004) suggest that:

> Knowledge management is about connecting to those who know the recipe more than capturing an encyclopedia of knowledge. Knowledge itself can be held in people's heads and it can be written down. Both sources should be used. It's about striking the right balance between people, process and technology. Knowledge is not just captured or shared, it is also created, discovered, distilled, validated, transferred, adopted, adapted and applied. Knowledge is richer than data and information; it's about familiarity gained from experience. (page 29)

There is an increasing emphasis on context-specific ('In our school we do it this way') and task-specific ('This how we solved this issue') knowledge. There is, however, also an inherent drift towards knowledge as being subjective and therefore not of general application, and a danger of wasteful reinvention and duplication. NCSL has countered this with its Three Fields of Knowledge model (see Figure 11.1). The strength of the model is that it allows for the creation of new knowledge without disconnection from the world of evidence-based research and becoming subjective. It also has huge power to build teams because of its inclusive dimension.

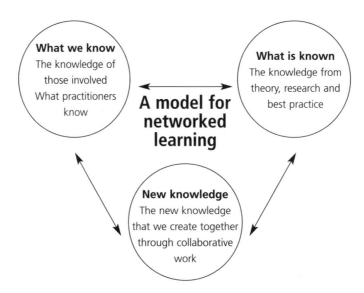

Figure 11.1 NCSL's Three Fields of Knowledge

Developing collaborative learning communities can take place using different pathways. There do seem to be some common phases and these are outlined in Figures 11.2 and 11.3. In the Team Restricted Learning phase there is collaboration and mutual learning within the Senior Leadership Team (SLT), which is disseminated to other school staff as policies, planning and projects. There is also some direct input into the school from consultants, LA advisory staff, etc. It is a limited model which could be described as a team-based hierarchy.

In the Institutional Diffusion Model, the boundary between the senior leadership team and the school staff has become more permeable. Staff are being listened to, their knowledge is being drawn into the decision making process and as a result there is increasing ownership of ideas. Typical of this phase were some of the outcomes from the TDA's remodelling initiative. At its heart was a change model with change teams drawn widely from within the school. The case study from the David Lister School, Hull (see page 84) exemplifies this increase in permeability with its development of change teams 'with teeth'.

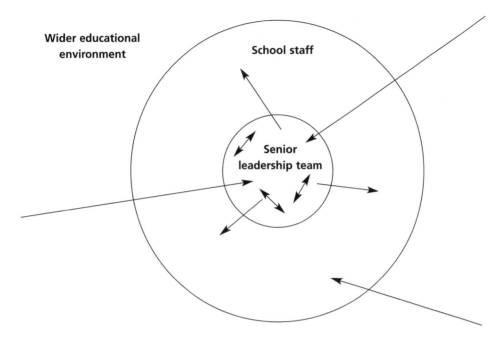

Figure 11.2 Team Restricted Learning

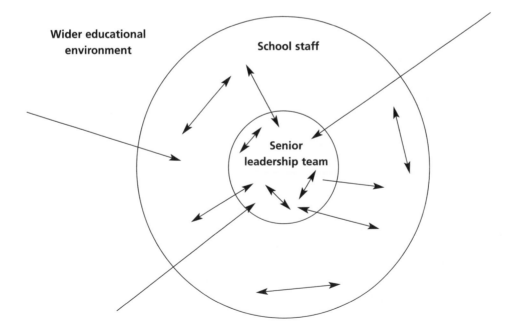

Figure 11.3 Institutional Diffusion Model

David Lister set up four change teams comprising over 30 teaching and non-teaching staff. The teams looked at ICT, the curriculum, Connexions and anything else that might raise standards.

Starting out

David Lister is a challenging school in the centre of Hull. It has successfully emerged, and indeed progressed, from special measures. The school's success has been accelerated by the work of four change teams, comprising over 30 teaching and non-teaching staff.

'The aim was to put staff in control of developing and implementing positive change,' says Steve Cook.

There was a conscious decision to include potential resisters as well as movers and shakers in each change team. This enabled teams to incorporate extra support into their plans to take account of the lack of confidence amongst some of their members.

[This is the reported outcome of just one of those teams.]

Collaborating with other schools

The school has developed a teaching and learning management open system (TALMOS) in collaboration with other secondary schools, the LEA and a local software engineering company. Advanced Skills Teachers (ASTs) and other teachers across the city are in charge of loading the system with work ideas and schemes (broken down into learning objectives), including a variety of introductions, 'main sections' and endings for every lesson.

Each learning objective has six options, taking into account different learning styles, and each lesson plan offers a variety of additional resources. This gives teachers a very accessible choice of high-quality lessons. The more straightforward work ideas and schemes can also be used by pupils at home and by supply teachers. TALMOS significantly reduces lesson planning time, allows less experienced or newly qualified teachers to plan as well as the best teachers, helps share good practice across schools, improves the quality of cover and raises pupils' standards.

The second phase process continues to develop but now the outer boundary of the school is becoming increasingly permeable with the wider educational community (see Figure 11.4). Of course schools have worked alongside other institutions and schools for many years. Arguably this is more developed as decision making draws on the knowledge of those outside the school community. The second part of The David Lister case study shows the school operating at a system level.

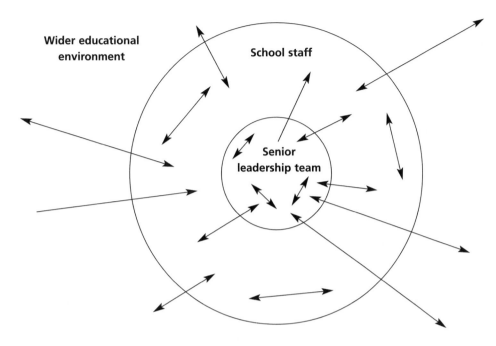

Figure 11.4 Knowledge creation at the level of the system

Blogging it

Collison and Parcell (2004) argue that there should be carefully considered mechanisms for sharing the knowledge that is being created. There are many imaginative ways of sharing learning; the difficult part is changing the culture to engage with the process. Louise Stoll (2004) has concluded that trust is at the heart of this process:

> The human side of bringing about any change or development is extremely important. Engaging in learning can be risky. It's not easy for people to open themselves up to participate in activities such as mutual enquiry, classroom observation and feedback, mentoring partnerships and discussion about pedagogical issues and innovation unless they are confident it is safe to do this. Trust is therefore a key condition and has been found in one study to be considerably the strongest facilitator of professional community. Along with respect, mutual support, celebration of success, and willingness to take risks, trust is one of the norms of a collaborative culture. (page 35)

Most schools have sophisticated ICT systems and yet the potential of using these as a focus for sharing learning within the organization is not being exploited. Just imagine, for example, developing a blog around the teaching of a challenging class or capturing learning around the development of a team. ICT is about collaboration, not merely dissemination.

Just do it

'Come to the edge,' He said. They said, 'We are afraid.' 'Come to the edge,' He said. They came. He pushed them . . . and they flew. (Guillaume Apollinaire)

Knowledge management has all the feel of yet another initiative. The term might be tainted with jargon; however, the process is not a novelty. Knowledge management is about capacity in the face of an explosion in knowledge for which the description 'exponential' seems inadequate. A failure to attend to the learning of groups and individuals in the organization spells disaster. Leadbeater (2004) has argued that organizations need to invest not only in new machinery to make production more efficient but also in the flow of know-how that will sustain their 'business'. Organizations need to be good at knowledge generation, appropriation and exploitation. We are not in the business of replication but of change and we need to share all the insights, wisdom and expertise as widely as possible. It is pre-eminently about collaboration to innovate and to increase effectiveness.

Collison and Parcell (2004) capture the urgency of this embryonic movement with their advocacy of 'just do it'. The cost of less than perfect knowledge capture and management pales into insignificance alongside the vision of an organization where its learning simply ebbs away.

12 Body of knowledge

Be careful about reading health books. You may die of a misprint. (Mark Twain)

Take care of your body with steadfast fidelity. The soul must see through these eyes alone, and if they are dim, the whole world is clouded. (Johann Wolfgang von Goethe)

Fit for purpose

Like many others I have been intrigued by the meteoric rise to fame of the young British racing driver Lewis Hamilton. On the face of it motor racing seems like a shortcut to sporting prowess. Formula 1 appears to offer the opportunity to dispense with effort and sweat and apply a few Newtons of force to the accelerator to draw down around 700 hp. This is, of course, very far from the truth. McLaren have a fitness centre and sports medical team supporting the track performance of their drivers. Hamilton and one-time teammate Alonso have each had a personal trainer. There is even a system of telemetry so that information about cardiovascular performance can be sent back to McLaren's database when drivers are in training elsewhere. This is a far cry from the 1960s when Jim Clark dined on steak and chips before major races.

In F1 the demands are extreme and the stakes are high. Leadership too is an extreme activity and fitness is not only about performance but also about personal health and wellbeing. If Hamilton were to become obese he would not fit into his car and would probably have his contract terminated. If a senior leader is obese or drinks heavily, even if the drinking is below the level of dependency, advice may possibly be given but sacking remains a remote possibility.

The Health and Safety Executive (2007) has produced excellent materials on work-related stress including an assessment tool. Earlier this year a consultant was working with a cluster of primary schools on wellbeing and stress. As a precursor this HSE analysis tool was used with the headteachers. All were found to be operating at unacceptably high levels of stress. Interestingly, when they received their results they cancelled a planned professional development day, even paying the agreed fee to the consultant. It is believed that there was a real fear that if the tests were replicated with other staff similar levels of stress would be revealed. If this were to be the case the legal fallout would have been considerable.

Leading schools is a demanding activity and is stressful. Stress, however, is a two-way street. On the one side there are links between high levels of stress and reduction in health (though some of these have not been fully substantiated). On the other hand, like Lewis Hamilton, fitness and positive mental state are linked to cognitive performance and personal capacity.

It would be a significant omission not to consider leadership and health and fitness. The following is intended to raise issues rather than serve as a definitive health guide, and should certainly not be seen as a substitute for informed medical advice by healthcare professionals, who will readily give guidance on issues such as weight, blood pressure, stress, depression, smoking and drinking. They should be seen as the first port of call and not the last chance saloon. Recently the front wheel fell off my son's car whilst he was driving down the M6. It is being repaired as I write (at some cost). Preventative maintenance or even stopping as the wobble started would have been a much better option than the debacle that followed.

The following case study was taken from a mentoring session, and again has been anonymized.

Case study: A leader of substance

John, a substantial man, greeted me at the start of the first mentoring session. He presented an avuncular style, which was betrayed by eyes that constantly scanned the perimeter. I was provided with the almost mandatory verbal business card: the school was Leading Edge, Specialist, Beacon, Training School, etc. Student achievement was excellent and sustained. I was thinking by this point, shall I just get my coat and leave!

We soon moved to the focus of our session, and indeed that of a number of our subsequent sessions together, federation. John is a well-respected and successful head. An informal collaboration between his school and two others had just broken down with the new head of one of the other schools deciding to go it alone. The remaining school had struggled for some years and the current head was retiring. John had been approached about the possibility of being the federated head of the two schools.

Clearly movement into system leadership was going to present significant issues and a redefinition of his role. He was very much aware that he could be drawn into becoming a traditional head in each of the schools. There was staffing, curriculum, budget and collaboration to bottom out and initially it appeared that the mentoring process was to be about redefining his new role.

What actually emerged were major concerns about his leadership capacity. Having just turned 50 he confided that whilst things were going well he was 'peddling ever harder' to keep up.

As the mentoring relationship developed a number of personal issues were disclosed about which he expressed anxiety. He was working long hours, in school at 7.30 am and usually leaving around twelve hours later, and even then taking work home. Most of life was being fitted in around the job and many activities which he had enjoyed, such as golf, had gone by the board. Eating was done on the run with little thought about nutrition and his weight had crept up significantly over the past ten years. Relaxation on reaching home usually consisted of having a couple of glasses of wine with his wife before starting work again.

John recognized that he often felt tired and irritable; underneath the confidence and undoubted competence was an anxious man. We discussed his perception of the situation. I explained that I was more than willing to look at some of the work–life balance issues. I also explained that I had come to an agreement with local medical practitioners that I did not practise medicine and in turn that they did not do educational consultancy. Furthermore, both parties were happy with this arrangement.

John agreed to get thoroughly checked out. It was quickly determined that he had developed type 2 diabetes. A resolute man, he acted on the advice.

Subsequently after (not over) an incredibly healthy lunch we tackled some of the complexities of system leadership.

The following is by no means an exhaustive list of health-related areas.

Weight

Our weight has a major impact on our health. Currently extremes of body size, whether the size-zero models or our national slide into obesity, have a regular place in the media. Statistically it is obesity which is most likely to be the common health issue for leaders. It is a very significant risk factor for health. Being overweight carries potential consequences of developing diabetes, coronary heart disease, raised blood pressure, strokes, strain on the joints, digestive disorders, cancer and liver problems. It also can reduce our stamina and confidence.

Over the past few years weight has been translated into the Body Mass Index (BMI), which links height, weight and body fat. BMI is usually categorized into bands or categories. These are the weight ranges currently set by the World Health Organization:

- If your BMI is less than 18.4 you're underweight for your height.
- If your BMI is between 18.5 and 24.9 you're an ideal weight for your height.
- If your BMI is between 25 and 29.9 you're over the ideal weight for your height.
- If your BMI is between 30 and 39.9 you're obese.
- If your BMI is over 40 you're very obese. (NHS Direct, 24/8/2007)

Another useful indicator is waist circumference measured around the navel (see Table 12.1).

	Increased risk	Substantially Increased risk
Men	Greater than 94 cm	Greater than 102 cm
Women	Greater than 80 cm	Greater than 88 cm

Table 12.1 Waist circumference and risk of coronary heart disease and type 2 diabetes (Waine, 2002, page 43)

Excessive weight carries severe penalties for our health. Whilst BMI charts are readily available in books and online your local health centre will be happy to advise you of the state of play and what to do about weight reduction.

Diet

A healthy diet is about both quantity and quality.

We have moved from post-war austerity towards 'eating for Britain'. Crucially our portion sizes have grown over the years. Like many who have been to the USA I was in awe of the size of the meals, I had breakfast one Sunday morning at 'Bob's Big Boys' restaurant. It was all there in the name. In Britain we are catching up fast. Many of us tend to underestimate the amount of food we eat and tend to overestimate the recommended portion sizes for many foods.

For example, try pouring out your usual portion of pasta and measure it! Then, compare it to the label portion size. Chances are, you're eating two, three, four or more times the amount on the label. Relating the portion size of a serving to everyday items is an easy way to visualize what a true portion size looks like. Consider the following:

- *woman's fist or rounders ball* – a serving of vegetables or fruit is about the size of your fist;
- *a rounded handful* – about half a cup of cooked or raw veggies or cut fruit, a piece of fruit, or half a cup of cooked rice or pasta – this is a good measure for a snack serving, such as chips;
- *deck of cards or the palm of your hand (don't count your fingers!)* – a serving of meat, fish or poultry, for example a chicken breast, a quarter of a pound of hamburger or a medium pork chop;
- *golf ball or large egg* – a quarter of a cup of dried fruit or nuts;
- *tennis ball* – about half a cup of ice cream;
- *computer mouse* – about the size of a small baked potato;
- *compact disc* – about the size of a serving of pancake or a small waffle;
- *thumb tip* – about a teaspoon of peanut butter;

- *six dice* – a serving of cheese;
- *cheque book* – a serving of fish (approximately 80 g/3 oz).

The quality of food that we eat is also crucial to our general health, survival and leadership performance. Our engagement with the Every Child Matters agenda has alerted us to the need to develop pupil understanding about healthy eating. The same principles apply to the Every Leader Matters agenda.

The following are a few of the headlines:

- Reduce your intake of salt.
- Reduce your intake of sugar.
- Eat five a day (fresh fruit and vegetables).
- Reduce your intake of saturated fats (limit red meat).
- Eat oily fish at least twice a week.
- Start the day with breakfast.
- Eat plenty of fibre.
- Drink plenty of water.

Obviously this is general advice and people with medical conditions or those who are pregnant should seek specialist advice.

Some years ago, at a school where I was the headteacher, we published a recipe book containing some provided by famous people. Tony Robinson (of Baldrick fame) sent us the recipe for 'Turnip au Naturelle' – 'dig up a turnip and eat it'. Perhaps there is a market for 'Recipes for Senior Leadership Teams'.

Exercise

The body is unusual in that unlike many machines it benefits from appropriate and regular use, which actually prevents deterioration. Exercise is a central part of a healthy lifestyle. Regular exercise helps to maintain fitness in terms of stamina but also our mobility and flexibility. It also helps to improve general health, circulation and posture, and supports mental state and positive thinking.

Marathon runners, joggers, salsa dancers and tri-athletes include many school leaders. Their very enthusiasm can send a shiver down the spine. I was recently talking to a marathon runner who was explaining how his feet bled for the last seven miles of the London Marathon! Some of us played competitive sport when we were younger and feel that we have passed our sell-by date. There is no way round our need for exercise but arguably stress will increase if we force ourselves to engage in activity that we feel we 'ought' or 'should' do. If you enjoy the gym that is fine but otherwise opportunist exercise can still be hugely beneficial. This might include walking to the shops, gardening, cycling and even using the stairs instead of lifts. Small changes soon add up and will improve your circulation and fitness level.

If you have not exercised regularly for a while then again it is important to seek medical advice before starting.

Alcohol consumption

Drinking alcohol is a bit like the way ivy grows up a house: it creeps. The occasional glass all too easily becomes the regular bottle.

Alcoholic drinks come in a phenomenal range of types: they vary in strength, flavour and colour. At the core of each is ethanol, which is a depressant of the nervous system and as such it will certainly not enhance your mood. As we all know, its progressive effects impact on motor control, speech, vision and in extreme cases consciousness and respiration. Whilst some drink for the taste, others value its narcotic effect and use it to smooth out the turbulence of the day.

Many organs can be affected by alcohol; however, it is usually the liver that pays the greatest price. The recommended weekly units have been offered largely in that organ's defence. Current wisdom from the Department of Health is that men should not regularly drink more than 3–4 units of alcohol per day, and women should not regularly drink more than 2–3 units of alcohol per day. After an episode of heavy drinking it is advisable to refrain from drinking for 48 hours to allow your body to recover. In fact it is recommended that we have an alcohol fast for two days each week anyway.

Technically a unit is 10 ml of pure alcohol. Most people know that a pint of ordinary strength lager or beer is two units. Perhaps fewer people realize that an ordinary glass of wine is also 2 units or that a bottle is 8 units. Be aware too that many wines and beers on sale have increased in strength over the past few years.

The key to understanding your drinking habits is honesty. Healthcare professionals maintain a cynical approach to the information that patients give them over their alcohol consumption.

Smoking

Smoking kills. If you're killed you've lost a very important part of your life. (Brooke Shields during an interview to become spokesperson for a federal anti-smoking campaign)

In some sense this quote sums up the problem of smoking. Continued smoking impairs the performance of every organ system in the human body. For teachers and school leaders there is the additional issue of the behaviour that is being modelled to pupils and students.

Considerable help is available to stop smoking. Again your local health centre is an extremely useful resource where specialist advice and support is available.

Relaxation

> During [these] periods of relaxation after concentrated intellectual activity, the intuitive mind seems to take over and can produce the sudden clarifying insights which give so much joy and delight. (Fritjof Capra)

Leadership can at times seem relentless and all-consuming. The stress generated draws our bodies into our experiences as well as occupying our thoughts – just ponder the phenomenon of the tension headache. We need to switch off, and this may well be by simply doing something different, for example the luxury of a soak in the bath or listening to music or even playing it. Many people find an external input beneficial such as massage, a sauna or yoga.

These activities are powerful allies because they not only create space but also engage our minds, senses and bodies. Being kind to ourselves is not selfish but an essential part of our portfolio of surviving and thriving.

Life–work balance

This is now enshrined in law in the School Teachers' Pay and Conditions Document 2004. This legislation requires that:

- additional hours over and above the annual 1,265 must be reasonable;
- for those teachers not covered by the 1,265 limit on directed time, overall hours must be reasonable;
- headteachers must have regard to the desirability of all teachers being able to achieve a satisfactory work–life balance;
- governing bodies are obliged to ensure that headteachers can achieve a reasonable work–life balance (www.nasuwt.org.uk, accessed 24/8/07).

This is genuinely commendable and certainly a step in the right direction. It does not, however, address three very significant areas:

1. Leaders, like teachers, work at different rates, some fast some slow. How we work is very much allied to our personality, and standards that are acceptable to one are inadequate to another. Consider the use of IT in the management of marking, data and the production of reports. For some teachers and leaders this is a timesaving approach whilst for others the system itself presents huge levels of challenge and takes inordinate amounts of time.

2. In any school there are core tasks to be undertaken and completed. Whilst poor management and leadership can add unnecessary burdens, these core tasks must be completed. Running a school is not in the same league as producing widgets (leaving the discussion about endogenous growth theory on one side), where a reduction in time simply means a reduction in output. Not completing the budget or not teaching a particular programme of study or deciding not to join the Ofsted process are options only for the terminally foolhardy. Obligatory tasks often fall back on to senior leaders.

3. Senior educational leaders have always understood their role as not legislatively time limited. Running a school is a pervasive activity and readily fills the mind from the early morning shower through to putting the cat out last thing at night. Hours can be legislated but you cannot legislate for percentage of headspace.

The task of leading a school will invade every hour available. There are times of particular pressure both throughout the year or on introducing a new initiative. The difficulty is that the exceptional soon becomes norm. Accepting that as mere mortals we are limited to 24-hour days, the only area that the job can extend into is our private space, and for many this means into our personal relationships and into family time. In turn this generates tension and guilt.

It is imperative that our life plan remains holistic and that we generate values and priorities for all areas of our lives. It may well be useful to explore our working practice and determine whether we are engaging with appropriate priorities (the 'urgent and important' and especially the 'not urgent and important'). Perhaps we need to develop new working practices and time management skills (see Chapter 7). Personal reflection is beneficial though many leaders see this as an indulgence. A good mentor can be of significant benefit in supporting your thinking through these issues. In Chapter 14 some guidance is offered for selecting a mentor.

Altering course

In *Personalizing Learning* (West-Burnham and Coates, 2005) the Readiness Capability Grid was outlined. It was used as a tool to consider where staff were placed in terms of readiness, in other words their commitment to the school's vision and values, and of capability, in other words the levels of knowledge and skills that individuals possessed in order to engage in new initiatives. The grid would also seem to be a useful tool to check where we are in terms of making personal life choices – see Figure 12.1 (reproduced by kind permission of Sage Publications).

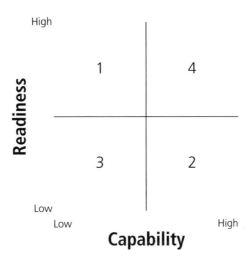

Figure 12.1 Readiness Capability Grid (after Everard and Morris, 1996, page 243)

Consider for a moment which of the four positions on the grid best represents your current situation:

1. *High readiness allied to low capability*. In essence you are committed to making changes but would benefit from some informed advice on how to make the required changes. Information or advice from a dietician, nurse or doctor might be extremely helpful.
2. *Low readiness coupled with high capability*. You understand the issues, you know the facts (or at least many of them) but you lack motivation to engage with the necessary change. Mentoring might help in exploring the possibilities and consequences of not taking action.
3. *Low readiness and low capability*. In his presentations on leadership John West-Burnham often described people in this category of low readiness and low capability as being 'the walking dead'. Sadly this could easily become prophetic. Change is unlikely as there is neither knowledge nor motivation. It may well take a significant life crisis like a stroke to initiate the desire to change.
4. *High readiness and high capability*. if you are in this category you have aligned both resources and personal commitment to take change forward. This is a powerful position to engage with personal change. The only caveat is that pressure can relegate this key area to a lesser priority and stall the change.

I am grateful to my wife, a senior practice nurse, for help in constructing this chapter and checking the information. The professional challenge that she faces is that many patients do not take responsibility for the lifestyle changes required to improve or to secure good health. It is vital that as leaders we are more Lewis Hamilton than Bernard Manning if we are to be both effective in our leadership role and also enjoy the fruits of our considerable hard work.

13 Buy one get one free

We are entering a new era in school leadership, which is challenging the long held assumption that every school needs its own headteacher. In future school leadership may not be about just leading individual institutions but about working in the wider system, although often still having one school as a base. So one person may be leading a number of schools or even a number of different children's centres or services across a local area. (Mumby, 2006, page 1)

Currently, system leadership is regarded as an elite practice, but if the aim is to improve learning by professionals working more closely across schools to lead reform, then system leadership must be turned into a national movement. (Hopkins, 2007, page 172)

It is not entirely clear how widely the term 'system leadership' is understood amongst school leaders. Many, even at senior leadership level, tend to greet its use with blank looks. If 'federated schools' are mentioned there is some connection, though this is misleading because clearly system leadership embraces but transcends this concept. For some, like David Hopkins (2007), system leadership is seen as a transformational process with the potential to take school improvement to new levels. Others, such as Steve Mumby (2006), recognize the pragmatic dimension facing schools as a leadership shortfall gathers momentum. Certainly the concept of system leadership represents a radical change but one which must always be seen in the wider context of workforce reform.

A metaphor

When I was a child my father took me to his work's open day. As well as the factory tour I was also shown the mainframe computer that the company had just bought. It was huge, entered by an airlock and the only movement was the large rotating tape reels. Because of the significant capital investment everybody, apart from perhaps the tea lady, had to make use of it. Systems such as invoicing had to be rewritten and put on it and stock control was transferred to its memory. Usage was strictly regulated and there were clearly defined time slots allocated to departments. Progressively the limitations and demands of the machine dictated the structure and function of the company itself. In the 1990s the PC began to be widely introduced and the desktop was able to handle many of the tasks previously handled by such digital leviathans. It did not take long for PCs to be networked both in cabled form and through the internet, each PC added to the system being inherently a user but also a resource.

In the 1980s and 1990s education became increasingly shaped by the demands of centralization in terms of curriculum, accountability, financial control, inspection, targets and even vision with the development of specialist schools. In the past five years an analogous process from the mainframe to the deployment of PCs has taken place. Power is increasingly being delegated to schools whilst at the same time the schools are beginning to inform and shape the system. For example the Innovation Unit has sponsored local initiatives to enhance learning at a system-wide level.

At present there are many developments in the area of system leadership. Some are largely structural, typically the federated school where the expertise of one head overarches several existing schools. There are also partnerships ranging from one school working alongside another to more elaborate town-wide partnerships like that evolving in Winsford, Cheshire.

David Hopkins (2007) explores the power of such aggregations in raising achievement arguing that the energy and expertise in success of one school can support another in challenging or transitional circumstances. Whilst he is a strong advocate of such developments at the local level, he retains a more circumspect vision of wider regional and national change. He argues that transformation can be underpinned by an approach to system leadership in three dimensions:

- System leadership at the school level – with, in essence, school principals becoming almost as concerned about the success of other schools as they are about their own.
- System leadership at the local/urban level – with practical principles widely shared and used as a basis for local alignment (across an urban area) so that school diversity and collaboration are deliberately exploited with specific programmes for the most at risk groups.
- System leadership at the national level – with social justice, moral purpose and a commitment to the success of every learner providing the focus for transformation through, in this instance, advocacy for school trusts. (Hopkins, 2007, page 173)

Case study: System leadership

This is a nursery school with a total enrolment of around 100 pupils. The senior leadership team comprises a headteacher, deputy head, nursery nurse coordinator and a programme manager. The nursery is situated in an area with significant pockets of social deprivation and is at the forefront of the government's strategy to integrate early years education, healthcare and family support. The Nursery School and Children's Centre operate in a new purpose-built centre in the middle of a housing estate, and is seen as a 'service hub' within the local community.

This is a nursery school with a total enrolment of around 100 pupils. The senior leadership team comprises a headteacher, deputy head, nursery nurse coordinator and a programme manager. The nursery is situated in an area with significant pockets of social deprivation and is at the forefront of the government's strategy to integrate early years education, healthcare and family support. The Nursery School and Children's Centre operate in a new purpose-built centre in the middle of a housing estate, and is seen as a 'service hub' within the local community.

In 2005 the headteacher was successful in a bid to participate in the Next Practice in System Leadership field trials. As part of the core services the centre provides early years education and childcare from 8 am to 6 pm for children aged from six months. The centre also offers a full range of other services including a childminder network; parent and toddler groups, a toy library and parenting programmes. In addition, the centre provides access to a range of other services including health services, training and support, and adult education.

The headteacher is clear about the benefits of Next Practice in System Leadership: 'It is about working in conjunction with children and families to meet their needs. Children and families are at the centre of everything we do – we like to say "yes".'

The need to develop an effective leadership and governance structure to enable the Nursery School and Children's Centre to manage the school provision, and the wider element of multi-agency working, was identified early on. It was thought that involvement in the field trial would support the Nursery School and Children's Centre in reshaping its governing structure; retaining an overall responsibility for leading activities on-site (including maintained nursery education for children aged 3–5, childcare for children aged 0–3, extended care, childminding networks and Families Aloud programmes); and delegating resources to an alliance of key services providing an essential link to support integrated service delivery of the wider ECM agenda.

A Community Alliance (which includes health and social services, police, local charities and other community representatives) has been created to achieve this. The headteacher of the nursery school will be responsible for the day-to-day running of on-site activities in the school, particularly those linked to the quality of education. In addition, the headteacher would be the lead member of the Community Alliance and agree the use of resources delegated to the alliance in liaison with key partners.

In July 2006 Ofsted reviewed the maintained nursery school provision and judged it to be

'outstanding'. The school is at the cutting edge of innovative practice as it juggles the demands of sustaining high quality education with those of its new and developing role as a children's centre. Even at this early stage, the impact of the leaders' vision and pioneering spirit can be seen in the seamless transition between under-threes provision and nursery education. (DfES and PricewaterhouseCoopers, 2007, page 63)

George W. Bush has been frequently criticized over his use of the phrase 'war on terror'. The implication of his words is that there is something out there which can be defined and attacked rather than 'terrorism' being a diffuse symptom of perceived injustices and poverty driven ideologies. In many ways to talk about 'system leadership' is to fall into the same trap. It is an emergent movement, which for some is rooted in ideology, whilst for others it has its origins in desperation. Hopkins gives an optimistic and well-argued advocacy of a potentially positive development. It is pertinent to keep in mind that this is a trend which is largely driven by the spectre of seven or eight years of leadership famine which has followed on from a similar period of feast.

Into the telephone kiosk

The lack of definition in the tasks of the system leader inevitably emerges as a lack of definition in the role. Whilst there are individuals who thrive on being pioneers and who do like to emerge out of the telephone kiosk like superman on a mission, many others work best within a defined remit.

Consider the scenario of becoming a federated head where there has been little joined-up thinking at the level of governance. Suddenly the number of meetings – governors', staff, parents' – has doubled to potentially two or more evening sessions per week. Assume for a moment that your time is equitably split between the schools and deputies are now being forced into an extended role as part-time heads, the very thing that the statistics quoted in the introduction to this book suggested that they wanted to avoid. It could be argued that succession is being secured by stealth.

Recently in working with Higher Level Teaching Assistants (HLTAs) I have encountered a great deal of anger from the perception that they are being used as cheap labour. Adding this perception to another layer within the school would be a significant mistake.

Hopkins (2007) actually pays scant attention to the nature of the leadership that would be required to take this process forward. He makes the assumption that the pool of such leaders would come from schools with an outstanding record of achievement. One of the attributes advocated is: 'Longevity of successful headship on the part of the lead school and a head who sees their success in the success of others and, crucially, who understands the process of school improvement' (Hopkins, 2007, page 162).

The underlying argument is that a successful school is inevitably led by a successful leader. For headteachers it is unpalatable to have to recognize how context-specific 'successful' leadership can often be. Circumstances can transform the competent leader into an apparently exceptional leader. There are many examples where success by a head in one school has been the prelude to disaster in another.

Just as there is no bounded definition to system leadership so there can be no generic skill set or list of competences. Consider the following scenarios:

1. Russell Green is a successful comprehensive school adjacent to Tilney Park, a school in special measures set in an area of social deprivation. Russell Green is asked to become the lead school in developing a redemptive partnership.

2. David Roberts has been the head of a successful school and for two years has been a lead player in a national project which is looking at developing innovative approaches to pedagogy. His absence has suited the aspirational deputy. However, the skills the latter has developed have now borne fruit in terms of the appointment as head of a nearby school.

3. Gravesbury is a small town which has decided to take its networked learning community to a new level and develop a common curriculum. The town has undergone demographic change with a reduction in the number of school-aged children. Initially it looked as if two of its schools might close. At the eleventh hour an influx of Eastern European families reversed this trend. The head of one of the primary schools is party to the development of a townwide 'umbrella' of education whilst responding to very changed circumstances as many of the children do not speak English and this school has taken on board the largest share of these children.

4. Rockwood is a medium sized comprehensive school which has committed itself to an area partnership. Simultaneously two problems have arisen: first, the school is on the boundary between two other local authorities and neighbouring schools are recruiting heavily. Second, a highly experienced deputy has had to have coronary bypass surgery and will be absent for a number of months.

Before exploring the requisite skill sets required for these situations there is a contextual prerequisite in each case, namely stable and supportive leadership within the 'sending' school. The heads of all of the schools are engaged in leadership beyond their own school, 'system leadership'. In the case of examples 2, 3 and 4 unforeseen circumstances have eroded the heads' support from within their own institutions. There is now a very real dilemma: do they continue with their wider leadership role or withdraw and refocus their efforts within their own schools? In many cases system leadership is developing outside of governance. It is often a selection of good ideas but ones which are separate to the 'proper job'.

High-performing schools can come 'off the boil' at frightening speed if circumstances change and appropriate leadership is not in evidence. In the case of example 2 the head had been so detached from leading his school that re-entry will prove to be extremely challenging.

Consider for the moment the skill set presented and the skill set needed for undertaking these wider roles:

1. The head of Russell Green has undoubtedly been successful. The key strategy employed was driving up achievement through the relentless use of data and holding staff to account. The school has enjoyed high levels of parental support and good pupil behaviour is a given. In terms of style the head is rather aloof and reserved and does not connect readily with his staff. He is supported by two very able deputies who provide the human face to this rather austere

leadership approach. Tilney Park, on the other hand, has poor levels of pupil discipline partnered by poor classroom practice. The staff see themselves as victims but are also united in their opposition to change. The leadership team have taken refuge in reactive management as opposed to strategic vision. I would suggest that the key skills required here are mentoring of the leadership ream, the development of behaviour management strategies and support in developing long-term planning. This lead head has a repertoire of authoritative leadership, data driven planning and handles relationships at a distance. Arguably there is a mismatch between need and provision.

2. National projects which seek to develop innovation require collaborative creative thinkers. David is a consummate committee member. Process readily replaces the project objectives. He is a detail person more interested in the frame than the picture itself. Credit must be given for his role in refining the output of the project, probably in the sense of being a Belbin style completer finisher. His main contribution is availability to the project as a consequence of the leadership capacity of his school.

3. The Gravesbury example actually has real potential to develop a system approach. Here the changing demography could have been dispersed through the system and the response has come from the network with collaboration in developing teaching and learning approaches for the immigrant/itinerant children. The key skill here is the ability to network and negotiate, though of course the context may not have been conducive as a result of other people's agendas.

4. Rockwood is more an issue of the capacity of the head to engage with the wider system. A further question is, what is this network actually about? Has it been formed because collaboration is held to be appropriate? Is it a political pressure group aligned against the local authority? Is it about two powerful secondary schools herding their associated feeder schools in order to secure transition?

On reflection

Senior leaders have routinely engaged with the wider system of education through meetings, working parties and committees. In a sense system leadership is about moving this to another level. Senge (1990) discusses change at an almost apocalyptic level whilst consideration here is altogether more modest. He does, however, provide two key indicators of system leadership:

> Two particular systems-thinking skills are vital: seeing patterns of interdependency and seeing into the future. It is one thing to say 'we are interdependent' and another to actually understand what this means specifically, especially for problems created by the present systems that no one knows how to solve. (page 1)

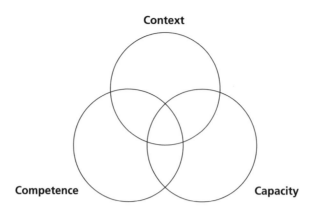

Figure 13.1 Dimensions of educational system leadership

I would suggest that engendering inter-dependence and engaging with the ambiguity of the future are germane to the system leader. Beyond these foundational commitments there are three fields relating to our current engagement with system leadership (see Figure 13.1).

Much has been made about the context of the system leadership development.

Like any other project its purpose must be explicit; it is not sufficient to be aspirational but should have appropriate terms of reference. Many projects will have significant political sensitivities so boundaries and protocols must be clear otherwise they will be a new forum for competitive dissent. Undoubtedly one of the key areas is that of governance, which must be integrated. Serving two masters has long been held to be untenable.

Capacity is unlikely to be an issue if the leadership role is formally constituted in that the appointment is to make the work in the system the primary focus. At this embryonic stage of system leadership key roles are more likely to evolve than to be designated. On the one hand, the willing can become overburdened whilst on the other, some individuals can seek control and dominance. Clearly neither scenario is to be welcomed. Where leaders enter into such an extended role they must be secure that their own school has the capacity to develop and thrive and that those who are participating by proxy are well informed and in agreement. This security about the support must be for the long term. Nothing less can sustain such extended professional engagement. All too often initial enthusiasm on the part of colleagues can deteriorate into resentment and even hostility. In turn initiatives do not benefit from an erratic lead as key players dip in and out.

I am always bewildered by that term 'designer clothes'. It always seems to beg the question as to whether other clothing was somehow an accident! In the same way, to talk about someone being a competent leader raises a frisson of concern. It is often an epithet awarded on a very subjective basis. Arguably there are no competent leaders; rather there are leaders who have developed a particular repertoire of leadership competences appropriate to a given context. In engaging with either the institution or the wider system these must be carefully matched with the task. A failure to do so will result in the individual undertaking a very steep learning curve, burning out or perhaps even worse limiting the initiative in line with their own skills.

Playing a formative role in the evolution of our education system and crafting the life chances of future generations is both demanding and energizing. Engagement requires a careful and considered analysis if personal dissolution is to be avoided. A regular refrain of this book has been about the potential benefits of appropriate mentor coaching and this area is no exception. An informative starting point is to undertake a personal leadership audit.

14 End game

It's very rare in a lonely job to have the time and be encouraged to talk about yourself, and not to an inspector or advisor or deputy, but to a fellow head . . . and for the first time in over 16 years of headship to feel that it's legitimate to do so. (Flintham, 2003a, page 27)

There are risks and costs to a programme of action. But they are far less than the long-range risks and costs of comfortable inaction. (John F. Kennedy)

I wrote this book out of a very real concern for colleagues in leadership in education. Very few lack commitment; many perhaps have too much. This book is about leading well but leading with regard to personal wellbeing. This concluding chapter is offered unashamedly as a challenge for leaders to engage in a process of personal review of their role as a leader. There are ten sections each of which requires a response. You may find it helpful to write down some of your conclusions and your intended actions.

Start a learning journal

If you are not learning you are unlikely to be leading effectively. A leadership learning journal is a useful adjunct. Simply using an A4 book to reflect on incidents, planning, and record vision, feelings and insights is a very powerful learning tool. The emphasis is always on what went well and how can my actions be even better.

Table 14.1 suggests some prompts which might be of help.

Reflecting on an incident	**Reflecting on a learning experience**
Describe an incident.	What were your expectations?
How did you feel?	What did you really want from the experience?
How were others feeling?	What did you learn?
What were the conditions or influences on what happened?	How did you learn?
Exactly what happened?	What opportunities or challenges did you face?
What was the chain of events?	Could you link the learning with your prior experience?
Was there more than one reason for the incident?	Will or did you act on the learning?
What other perspectives might pertain?	How did you feel about the experience?
What were the consequences?	Did others learn the same things in the same way?
What principles underpinned your actions?	What are your personal targets?
What professional issues were at stake?	Has there been progress in relation to personal targets?
What did you learn about yourself?	
What did you learn about others?	
What might others have learned about you?	

Table 14.1: Prompts for a leadership learning journal (after New Visions (2003), NCSL)

As an initial task reflect and then write down three learning points that have impacted on you from this book.

The listening leader

Select three staff from your school, preferably ones that you have not been working closely with. Arrange to see them individually and ask them to tell you about their work in the school. Ask about what they enjoy, what they are excited about, what opportunities or project they would like to develop.

Your task is to listen; it is amazing what you will find out about the school you know so well! Crucially it is about your listening. Ask questions for information but do not be tempted to interrupt or explain how things really are to the person.

Note down what has struck you about what the person was saying about his or her experience of the school and also how you found the experience of listening.

Record your story

On tape or disk take 15 minutes to tell the story of your school and your role in leading it. It sometimes helps to imagine that you are talking to somebody in the room. Ask a friend to listen to it with you. A suitable person would be someone whom you can trust, who is perceptive but not involved with the school.

Ask him or her to note down three areas:

1. Was your story framed negatively or positively (consider their response in the light of Chapter 3)?
2. How are you using language? Do you use hyperbole, for example 'everyone', 'all the time' and 'always'?
3. What priorities, issues of importance, emerge from the story you are telling?

Reflect with them on the nature of your story and its potential impact.

Implement one initial learning process with your team

Explain to your team that you intend to review the meeting at the end and budget time for the process and then probably double the time that you have allocated.

The technique suggested is an 'After Action Review' (AAR). This has its roots with the US army. In fact the AAR does not have to be performed at the end of a project or activity; rather, it can be performed after each identifiable event within a project or major activity, thus becoming a live learning process. The AAR is a professional discussion that includes the participants and focuses directly on the tasks and goals. It is not a critique. In fact, it has several advantages over a critique:

- It does not judge success or failure.
- It attempts to discover why things happened.
- It focuses directly on the tasks and goals that were to be accomplished.

- It encourages employees to surface important lessons in the discussion.
- More employees participate so that more of the project or activity can be recalled and more lessons can be learned and shared.

At the heart of AAR are four basic questions:

1. What was supposed to happen?
2. What actually happened?
3. Why were there differences?
4. What can we learn from this?

Note down the learning points and review these at the start of the next session.

Choose a mentor

This is a very brief review of a surprisingly complex activity. There is not enough space here to explore the subtleties between a mentor and a coach. Dr Jan Roberston (2005) summarized the underlying role neatly as:

> a special, sometimes reciprocal relationship between (at least) two people who work together to set professional goals and achieve them. The term depicts a learning relationship, where participants are open to new learning, engage together as professionals equally committed to facilitating each other's leadership learning and wellbeing (both cognitive and affective), and gain a greater understanding of professionalism and the work of professionals. (page 24)

There are many people who describe themselves as mentors or coaches. Regrettably many have simply rebranded themselves and actually operate from an old fashioned model of consultancy where telling has remained the core skill.

West-Burnham and Coates (2006) drew six conclusions on mentors:

1. They possess expertise and specialised knowledge in two important respects: Their role for example in learning and teaching or leadership. Support for the learning of others.
2. They make sense of their own knowledge and experience – they have sophisticated models and schemata that allow them to work intuitively, in other words, they have created personal meaning and wisdom.
3. Their mentoring skills are similarly intuitive: they exhibit automacity and are unconsciously competent.
4. Expert mentors are highly perceptive and skilled problem solvers. They have higher order analytical skills that allow them to understand a situation and generate appropriate and valid strategies.
5. They are highly reflective, constantly monitoring their own practice, seeking feedback on their performance as mentors and continually developing the repertoire of strategies to support and sustain their reflection.

6. Mentors are inclusive: they listen and negotiate, and they seek analysis and strategies before proposing, let alone imposing, solutions. (page 88)

A poor mentor is like a cheap suit: this provides an illusion of style but has no lasting quality.

Formulate your own mission statement

Generate your own personal mission statement relevant to your role as a leader. It should be between 10 and 15 words in length. Stephen Covey (1999) described four categories of leadership activity, which form a useful basis for analysis:

1. *Urgent and important* – those things which simply cannot be deferred, for example interviewing for appointments, teaching, organizing a parents' evening, dealing with an injured pupil.
2. *Not urgent but important* – these would include a task like development planning or changing the leadership structure. If it does not happen immediately the school does not stop; however, if vision and strategic development are not addressed the school will become moribund.
3. *Urgent but not important* – in general these seem to be the priorities others have for us.
4. *Not urgent and not important* – these are displacement activities; they have the appearance of busyness but little outcome. Frequently senior leaders get drawn into working parties or meetings, which realistically have little purpose.

Draw out a simple quadrant diagram and list activities that you have recently done or are currently doing in the appropriate section. Review these against your personal mission statement and explore the match and mismatch.

Review your time management system (or indeed start one)

Review your use of a:

- diary
- planner
- storage of information
- desk.

Perhaps ask the following questions:

- Can you rely on it or do you have to use a mental back-up system?
- Is it holistic – are all areas of your life organized 'under one roof'?
- Am I making time available to review and update my time management processes?

- Do I understand the type of person that I am, for example detail or a big picture thinker, and have I taken this into account as to how I organize my life?

Communications

Consider the checklist in Figure 14.1 and review some of the recommendations for the 'taming' of IT in the frame of your leadership.

Action	Completed
Budget time to answer emails just as you do for the post	
Have four email addresses	
Empty your inbox	
Separate attachments from emails	
Set email check to a minimum of 60 minutes	
Establish protocol for the use of distribution lists	
Ban the use off 'reply to all' function	
Have email free Fridays	
Write brief emails	
Set up email folders	
Have a business and a personal mobile	
Remove your mobile number from your business card	
Restrict the number of people with your mobile number	
Switch off your mobile for most of the day	

Figure 14.1 IT management checklist

Health check

Arrange an appointment for a check-up with your local doctor. This is often done under the guise of a 'well-woman' or 'well-man' clinic. It will usually check your weight (BMI), blood pressure, urine for diabetes and review health-related issues such as drinking, smoking and exercise.

Many of us are put off from doing this because we are frightened we might be told something we do not want to hear. In fact most health issues can be resolved with action and support.

Book a massage

Many people find this hugely relaxing. Please choose with care and ensure that it is a proper facility or the good intentions of this chapter could end with your career in tatters! At the heart of this suggestion is actually being kind to yourself and celebrating your self-value. Frequently senior leaders give altruistically to others to their own detriment.

End note

I would like to return to my initial theme of change, which I have argued is all-pervasive and accelerating. Leadership is about being part of communities of innovation engaging with others to forge new paths, but also being offered a hand when the terrain is uneven. There is no 'satnav' available to leaders to follow new routes but there are many who believe an about-turn might lead to previously well-trodden pathways. Sadly these old pathways lead back to the ruins of former times. Capra (2002) captures the tension of this leadership journey:

> The experience of the critical instability that precedes the emergence of novelty may involve uncertainty, fear, confusion or self-doubt. Experienced leaders recognise these emotions as integral parts of the whole dynamic and create a climate of trust and mutual support.
>
> During the change process some of the old structures may fall apart, but if the supportive climate and the feedback loops in the network of communications persist, new and more meaningful structures are likely to emerge. When that happens, people often feel a sense of wonder and elation, and now the leader's role is to acknowledge these emotions and provide opportunity for celebration. (page 108)

Leadership success is about succession and beyond. Of course the legacy of good leadership includes a well-run achieving school; however, the greater legacy is propagating leaders.

These will be men and women who have understood that contemporary leadership is about nurturing the next generation of leaders, who will outgrow them:

> The ultimate leadership contribution is to develop leaders in the organisation who can move the organisation even further after you have left. (Fullan, 2001, page 134)

References

Ambady, N., Laplante, D., Nguyen, T. et al. (1997) 'The relationship with malpractice claims among primary care physicians and patients', *Journal of the American Medical Association*, 277, 553–9 (abstract)

Barnett, B. (1995) 'Developing reflection and expertise: can mentors make the difference?' *Journal of Educational Administration*, 33 (5), 45–59

Barth, R. (2003) *Too Busy to Learn*, Nottingham: NCSL

Beaumont, C. (2007) 'The curse of the inbox overload', *Daily Telegraph*, 16 August

Belbin, R.M. (1981) *Management Teams*, New York: Wiley

Blagov, P.S., Westen, D., Harenski, K., Kilts, C. and Hamann, S. (2006) 'Neural bases of motivated reasoning: an FMRI study of emotional constraints on partisan political judgment in the 2004 U.S. presidential election', *Journal of Cognitive Neuroscience*, November

Bowden, B. (1969) The Language of Computers, Richard Goodman Memorial Lecture, Brighton College of Technology, www.chilton-computing.org.uk (accessed 20/8/2007)

Boyatzis, R. and McKee, A. (2005) *Resonant Leadership*, Boston, MA: Harvard Business School Press

Brighouse, T. (2003) *Values and Leadership in Education*, Nottingham: NCSL

Burnham, D. (2003) Prime Motives, People Management, www.burnrose.com/ (accessed 19/7/2007)

Capra, F. (2002) *The Hidden Connections*, London: HarperCollins

Collins, J. (2001) *Good to Great*, London: Random House Business Books

Collison, C. and Parcell, G. (2004) *Learning to Fly*, Chichester: Capstone Publishing

Cooperrider, D.L., Whitney, D. and Stavros, J. (2003) *Appreciative Inquiry Handbook*, Bedford Heights, OH: Lakeshore Publishers

Covey, S. (1999) *The 7 Habits of Highly Effective People*, London: Simon & Schuster

Csikszentmihalyi, M. (1990) *Flow: The Classic Work on How to Achieve Happiness*, London: Rider

De Bono, E. (2000) *Six Thinking Hats*, London: Penguin

Department for Education and Skills and PricewaterhouseCoopers (2007) *Independent Study into School Leadership*, London: DfES and PricewaterhouseCoopers

De Pree, M. (1990) *Leadership is an Art*, New York: Doubleday

Dijksterhuis, A. and van Knippenberg, A. (1998) 'The relation between perception and behaviour, or how to win a game of trivial pursuit', *Journal of Personality and Social Psychology*, 69 (5)

Eaton, J. (2006) *Reverse Therapy for Health*, San Francisco: Creative Commons

Ekman, P. and Friesen, W. (1978) *Facial Action Coding System Parts 1 and 2*, University of California, Berkeley

Elliott, R. and Tyrrell, M. (2003) *The Depression Learning Path*, Brighton: Uncommon Knowledge

Everard, K.B. and Morris, G. (1996) *Effective School Management*, 3rd edn, London: Paul Chapman

Flintham, A. (2003a) *Reservoirs of Hope*, Nottingham: NCSL

Flintham, A. (2003b) *When Reservoirs Run Dry*, Nottingham: NCSL

Friedman, T. (2005) *The World Is Flat: The Globalized World in the Twenty-First Century*, London: Penguin

Fullan, M. (2001) *Leading in a Culture of Change*, San Francisco: Jossey-Bass

Gladwell, M. (2005) *Blink: The Power of Thinking Without Thinking*, London: Penguin

Goleman, D. (1996) *Emotional Intelligence*, London: Bloomsbury Publishing

Goleman, D. (2006) *Social Intelligence: The New Science of Human Relationships*, London: Hutchison

Goleman, D., Boyatzis, R.E. and McKee, A. (2002) *The New Leaders: Transforming the Art of Leadership into the Science of Results*, London: Little, Brown

Griffin, J. and Tyrrell, I. (2004) *Human Givens: A New Approach to Emotional Health and Clear Thinking*, Chalvington, East Sussex: HG Publishing

Health and Safety Executive (2007) *Work Related Stress*, www.hse.gov.uk (accessed 13/8/07)

Heinlein, R. (1953) *Assignment in Eternity*, n.p.: Fantasy Press

Hock, D. (1999) *Birth of the Chaordic Age*, San Francisco: Berrett-Koehler

Holmes, T.H. and Rahe, R.H. (1967) 'Holmes–Rahe life changes scale', *Journal of Psychosomatic Research*, 11, 213–18

Hopkins, D. (2007) *Every School a Great School*, Maidenhead: Open University Press

Janis, I. (1972) *Victims of Groupthink*, Boston, MA: Houghton Mifflin

Katzenbach, J. and Smith, D. (2004) 'The discipline of teams', in Harvard Business Review (ed.) *Teams that Succeed*, Boston, MA: Harvard Business School, pp. 1–26

Kelly, K. (2005) We Are the Web, www.wired.com/wired/archive/13.08 (accessed 12/4/2007)

Kennedy, H. (2007) Lecture given for The Innovation Unit, Central Hall, Westminster (27/6/2007)

Lawson, M. (2000) 'A man of ideals', *Guardian*, 11 September

Leadbeater, C. (2004) *Learning about Personalisation*, Nottingham: DfES

Levinson, W., Roter, D.L., Mullooly, J.P., Dull, V.T. and Frankel, R.M. (1997) 'Physician–patient communication: the relationship with malpractice claims among primary care physicians and surgeons', *Journal of the American Medical Association*, 277 (7), 39–58

Lord, C., Ross, L. and Lepper, M. (1979) 'Biased assimilation and attitude polarization: the effects of prior theories on subsequently considered evidence', *Journal of Personality and Social Psychology*, 37, 2098–109

Maccoby, M. (2001) 'Narcissistic leaders: the incredible pros, the inevitable cons', in Harvard Business Review (ed.) *What Makes a Leader*, Boston, MA: Harvard Business School, pp. 27–52

Mumby, S. (2006) *Talk 2 Learn*, 19 May 2006 (accessed 27/8/2007)

National College for School Leadership (2006) *Leadership Succession: An Overview Securing the Next Generation of School Leaders*, Nottingham: NCSL

National Union of Schoolmasters Union of Women Teachers (2004) *School Pay and Conditions*, www.nasuwt.org.uk (accessed (24/8/2007)

Pert, C. (1997) *Molecules of Emotion*, New York: Scribner

Radford, T. (2003) 'Too good to be true', *Guardian*, 13 November

Robertson, J. (2005) *Coaching Leadership: Building Educational Leadership Capacity through Coaching Partnerships*, Wellington: NZCER Press

Senge, P.M. (1990) *The Fifth Discipline: The Art and Practice of the Learning Organization*, London: Random House

Southworth, G. (2004) *How Leaders Influence What Happens in Classrooms*, Nottingham: NCSL

Srull, T.K. and Wyer, R.S. (1979) 'The role of category accessibility in the interpretation of information about persons: some determinants and implications', *Journal of Personality and Social Psychology*, 37, 1660–72

Steele, C. and Aronson, J. (1995) 'Stereotype threat and intellectual test performance of African Americans', *Journal of Personality and Social Psychology*, 69 (5), 87–106

Stoll, L. (2004) *Networked Learning Communities as Professional Learning Communities*, Nottingham: NCSL

Strack, F., Martin, L. and Strepper, S. (1988) 'Inhibiting and facilitating conditions of the human smile: a non-obtrusive test of the facial feedback hypothesis', *Journal of Personality and Social Psychology*, 54, 768–76

Taylor, C. (1991) *The Ethics of Authenticity*, Cambridge, MA: Harvard University Press

Toffler, A. (1970) *Future Shock*, London: Bodley Head

Toffler, A. and Toffler, H. (2006) *Revolutionary Wealth*, New York: Knopf Publishers

Training and Development Agency (2003) *The David Lister School, Hull, Case Study*, www.tda.gov.uk (accessed 10/8/2007)

Tuckman, B.W. (1965) 'Developmental sequence in small groups', *Psychological Bulletin*, 63, 384–99

Veen, W. (2006) *Homo Zappiens: Growing Up in a Digital Age*, London: Network Continuum Education

Waine, C. (2002) *Obesity and Weight Management in Primary Care*, London: Blackwell Science

West-Burnham, J. (2002) *Leadership and Spirituality: Leading Edge Seminar Thinkpiece* Nottingham: NCSL

West-Burnham, J. (2003) *Moral Leadership*, Nottingham: NCSL

West-Burnham, J. and Coates, M. (2005) *Personalizing Learning: Transforming the Education for Every Child*, Stafford: Network Educational Press

West-Burnham, J. and Coates, M. (2006) *Transforming Education for Every Child: A Practical Handbook*, Stafford: Network Educational Press

Index

Aaronson   19
action   73
adrenaline   29, 30, 31
Advanced Skills Teachers
   (ASTs)   84
affirmations   45
African-American Caribbean
   Students   19
After Action Review (AAR)
   106, 107
air traffic controllers   14
alcohol   92
'all or nothing' thinking   19
Ambady, N.   28
ambiguity   18
anecdotes   12,17
anterior cingulated cortex   11
antidepressants   30, 31
Apple   55
Appreciative Inquiry (AI)   76
Aronson, J.   42
assembly   13
asymmetric communication
   14

Bach, R.   44
Bandler, R.   42
Barth, R.   54
BBC   5
BBC Master 128   55
Beauchamp, G.   9
Beaumont, C.   58
Belbin, M.   62, 64, 65, 101
Blackberry   59
Blagove, P.S.   22
blood pressure   89
Blunkett, D.   5

body language   14
Body Mass Index (BMI)   89,
   110
bodymind   28
Bonaparte, N.   16
Boston   17
Boyatzis, R.   24
brain   12, 22
Brighouse, T.   37
Building Schools for the
   Future   8
Burham, D.   63
burnout   24
Burt, Sir Cyril   4
Bush, G.   22

cardiovascular performance
   87
Cambridge   2
capacity   102
Capra, F.   93, 110
Case Western University   76
cerebral cortex   27
change   1, 7, 8
change   63
Chesterton, G.K.   9
children's centers   96, 98
Christian imperative   40
Church of England   36
Churchill, W.   6
circle of excellence   47
coaching   68
Coates, M.   4, 78, 94, 107
cognitive behaviour therapy
   31
cognitive intelligence   29
collaboration   85, 101

Collins, J.   67
Collison, C.   79, 81, 86
communication   9, 11, 109
Community Alliance   98
competence   102
confirmation bias   22
connectivity   56
Connexions   84
context   102
conversation   11, 14
Cooperrider, D.   76, 77, 78
cortisol   29, 30
counsellors   15
Covey, S.   108
creative thinking   75
Csikszentmihalyi, M.   23, 32
curriculum   2, 36
cycle   24, 25
Cycle of statement, belief and
   action   43

David Lister School   82, 84
De Bono, E.   75
de Pree, M.   80
deep listening   12
delegation   31
delivery   78
Denning, S.   16
Department of Health   92
depression   27, 30
deputy   69
design   77
desk   53
diabetes   110
dialogue   37
diary   51
diet   90

Dijksterhuis   18
discovery   77
dopamine   22
dream   77
Dylan, B.   1

early years education   98
Eaton, J.   28, 29
ECM   98
Edison, T.   45
Educational Reform Act   63, 72
educationalists   8
egalitarian imperative   40
Einstein, A.   70
Ekman, P.   10
Elliot, R.   19, 20, 30, 31
email   59, 59, 109
emotion (s)   10, 11, 22
emotional brain   11, 29
emotional intelligence   28
emotional memories   27
emotional reactions   11
emotional state   9
empathic communication   12
empathy   12, 67
Encarta   4
Encyclopaedia Britannica   4
energy   27
enlightenment   1
Erikson, M.   42
erotic   67
ethics   34
ethnicity   19
Everard, K.   95
Every Child Matters   91
exercise   91

Facial Action Coding System
   (FACS)   10
facial expression   10, 11, 14
facial language   11
facial muscles   10
federated head   99
federated school   97
Fish, T.   13
Flintham, A.   16, 20,24, 39, 104
fMRI   22
FMSiS   49
focus   72
Ford, H.   62
Freud, S.   5
Friedeg, T.   5
Friedman, T.   55, 56

Friesen, W.   10
Fullan, M.   33, 64, 111
Future Shock   3

generational imperative   40
Gladwell, M.   28
globalization   2
Goleman, D.   6, 9, 12, 28, 57
Good Book   21
Good to Great   67
governing body   17
governors   18
governors' meeting   18
Graduate Record
   Examination   19
Grinder   42
GROW   68
Guardian, the   9
guitar   9

Hamilton, L   87, 88, 95
Hamlet   22
Hartree, D.   2
Head on the Block   5
headmind   27, 29, 30, 99
headteacher   10, 13, 14, 17, 20,
   69
health   110
Health and Safety Executive
   (HSE)   87
Heinlein, R.   21
heliotropic hypothesis   78
Herald Tribune, The   59
Hewlett Packard   3
Higher Level Teaching
   Assistant (HLTA)   99
hippocampus   28
Hock,   1–2,
Holmes, T.   25
hope   20
Hopkins, D.   96, 97, 99
Houston   70
Hull   82
humans   11
hypothalamus   28, 30

iPod   57
IBM   3, 55
illiterate   7
inbox   58, 59, 109
induction   9
information   51, 53
information and
   communication technology
   (ICT)   4, 55, 56, 82, 85, 86

information technology (IT)
   48, 51, 52, 55, 93
inner dialogue   12
innovation   7
Institutional Diffusion
   Model   82
interaction styles   14
interactions, verbal   13
interactions, non-verbal   13,
   14
Internet   3
interviewing panels   6
IQ   4
Islington Arts and Media
   School   5

Janis, I.   62
Japanese   3

Keate, Dr   33
Kelly, K.   56
Kennedy, H.   79
Kennedy, J.F.   6, 104
Kerry, J.   22
knowledge capture   79
knowledge creation   85
knowledge management   7,
   79, 81
Katzenbach, J.   63, 64

Lawson, M.   5
lead learners   80
Leadbeater, C.   86
leader – narcissistic   6, 7
leader – balanced   6
leader(s)   5, 8, 21, 80, 93, 94,
   104, 105
leaders senior   101
leadership   5, 14, 99, 100, 110
leadership – erotic   5
leadership – narcissistic   5
leadership – obsessive   5
leadership, system   96, 97,
   100, 101, 102
Leading from the Middle   28,
   46
learning – students   8
learning journal   53, 104,
leisure and tourism   2
Levinson, W.   28
life–work balance   93
Life Change Units   24, 26, 27
limbic centre   11

limbic system   29
listening   105
London Challenge   73
Lord   21

Machiavelli   66
Maccoby, M.   5, 50
manager (s)   5,17
Manchester   2
massage   110
McKee, A.   24
McLaren   87
memory   97
mentor-coaching   103
mentor   17, 23, 107, 108
mentoring   17
metaphor   8
midbrain   28
Milgram, S.   16, 17
mirror neurons   11
mobile phone   60, 109
modelling   37
monitoring   37
morals   34
Morris, J.   95
Motivational Mapping   68
MSN   57
Mumby, S.   96

narcissistic   67
   leader   6, 7
   leadership   5
National College for School
   Leadership   24, 34, 46, 68,
   105
National Curriculum   4
National Professional
   Qualification for
   Headship   28, 48
nerve cells   11
Neuro-Linguistic
   Programming (NLP)   42,
   46, 47
New Visions   75, 105
New York Times, The   79
Newtonian   2
Next Practice   98
norepinephrene   30
nursery school   97, 98

obesity   89
obsessive   67
Ofsted   35, 72, 98
Omaha   16

open-loop   49
open door   14
orbitofrontal area   11
organization   2

Parcell, G.   79, 81, 86
pedagogy   36
perception   17, 18
personal computer (PC)   55,
   97
Personal Digital Assistant
   (PDA)   49, 51, 52
Pert, C.   18
planner   52
Popular Mechanics   2
post-industrial   7
prefrontal cortex   11, 27
pressure   7
primates   11
problem   70
Problem Solving Team
   Building (PSTB)   73, 74, 75
psychologist(s)   16, 21
purpose   62, 63, 64
Pygmalion Effect   78

Radford, T.   4
Rahe, R.   25
Raskin, J.   55
Readinesss/Capability Grid
   94, 95
relationships   17, 66
relaxation   31, 93
reflective practitioner   7
Renaud   58
Reservoirs of Hope   16, 20
resonance   9
review   53
Revolutionary Wealth   3
Rickenbacker, A.   9, 10
Robertson, J.   107
Rolls Royce   8

scanning   13
school climate   13
School Improvement
   Partners   24
School Teachers' Pay and
   Conditions (2004)   93
schools   12
self-talk   43, 44
Senge, P.   80, 101
senior leaders   21, 57, 81

senior leadership team   82, 83,
   85
seratonin   30
Shakespeare   22
Sharon, Massachussetts   17
Shefffield Simplex   8
six degrees of separation   17
Six Thinking Hats   75
Smith, D.   63, 64
smoking   92
solution   73
Southworth, G.   36, 37
spindle cells   11
Srull, T   41
Staubach, R.   62
Steele, C.   19, 42
Stoll, L.   85
story   16, 22, 106
Strack, F.   10
stress   23, 30, 60
strider heads   24
stroller heads   24
stumbler heads   24
subordinates   6
succession   7
superheads   5
SWOT   66
sycophants   7, 21
sympathy   12

Taylor, C.   40
team(s)   7, 64, 65, 69, 79
Team Restricted Learning   82
teams leadership   64
teams, dysfunctional   62
teams, project   63
teamwork   7
Teddington   2
Telstar   59
temporal lobes   27
Three Fields of Knowledge
   81, 82
tickler file   53
time management   50, 94, 108
Times Educational
   Supplement   35
Toffler, A.   3, 7, 57
Toffler, H.   3, 7, 57
Training and Development
   Agency (TDA)   73, 74, 79,
   82
transference imperative   4040
transition   1, 5, 7
Trivial Pursuit   18

trust   85
Tuckman, B.   62
Twynham School   13
Tyrell, M.   19, 20, 30, 31

units of alcohol   92
University of Glasgow   57
US army   106

value system   40
values   7, 33, 34, 35, 39
van Knippenberg   18

Veen, W.   56
vocational imperative   40

Waine, C.   90
waist circumference   90
weight   89
wellbeing   104
West-Burnham, J   4, 20, 33,
    34, 36, 78, 94, 107
White, T.   77
Wikipedia   4
Windows   55

work–life balance   93
Working Together for
    Success   68
World Health Organization
    89
World Wide Web   3, 56
Wurzburg   10
WWW/EBI   68
Wyer, R.   41

Yoda   41